MEDITATIONS
ON THE
PARABLES OF JESUS

OTHER BOOKS BY THOMAS KEATING

Journey to the Center

The Heart of the World:
An Introduction to Contemplative Christianity

Intimacy with God:
An Introduction to Centering Prayer

Crisis of Faith, Crisis of Love

Open Mind, Open Heart

The Mystery of Christ:
The Liturgy as Spiritual Experience

Invitation to Love:
The Way of Christian Contemplation

Awakenings

Reawakenings

The Kingdom of God Is Like...

The Fruits and Gifts of the Spirit

Manifesting God

The Human Condition:
Contemplation and Transformation

The Better Part: Stages of Contemplative Living

MEDITATIONS
ON THE
PARABLES OF JESUS

BY THOMAS KEATING

A CROSSROAD BOOK
The Crossroad Publishing Company
New York

This printing: 2019

The Crossroad Publishing Company
www.crossroadPublishing.com

Project Management by
The Crossroad Publishing Company
John N. Jones

For this edition, numerous people have shared their talents and ideas. We thank especially:

Acquisition: The Crossroad Publishing Company
Cover design: Einat Blum
Text Design: Eve Vaterlaus
Editing and proofreading: Sylke Jackson

Concept, idea, development of text and
package, and market positioning by
The Crossroad Publishing Company

Library of Congress Cataloging-in-Publication Data is available from the Library of Congress.

ISBN-13: 978-0-8245-26078 (paper)

Books published by The Crossroad Publishing Company may be purchased at special quantity discount rates for classes and institutional use. For information, please email sales@crossroadpublishing.com.

MIX
Paper from
responsible sources
FSC® C004071

TABLE OF CONTENTS

PUBLISHER'S NOTE vii

FOREWORD viii
by Bernard Brandon Scott

AUTHOR'S PREFACE xi

PART I. GOD DWELLS IN THE ORDINARY

1. THE PUBLICAN AND PHARISEE 2
"The sacred has moved to everyday life."

2. THE MUSTARD SEED 5
*"We do not have to wait for an apocalyptic deliverance.
The kingdom is available right now."*

3. THE LOST COIN 13
*"There is no place to go to find the kingdom because
it is always close at hand."*

4. THE LEAVEN 1 19
"Look for the kingdom in the most unexpected places."

5. THE LEAVEN 2 25
*"The kingdom of God manifests itself in solidarity with other peo-
ple, in sympathy with their misfortune, and in unconditional love."*

6. THE LEAVEN 3 30
*"A difficult situation can be a great blessing, an opportunity
for God to heal us at the deepest level."*

7. THE LEAVEN 4 36
*"Our ideas of God and the kingdom need to be expanded
and to grow continuously."*

8. THE BARREN FIG TREE 41
*"The God of pure faith is closer than breathing, closer than think-
ing, closer than choosing, closer than consciousness itself."*

PART II. GOD LOVES INFINITELY AND ALWAYS

9. THE PRODIGAL SON 1 50
*"True security, independence, and affection
were all present in his father's house."*

10. THE REIGN OF GOD 1 55
(The Hidden Treasure, The Pearl, and The Net)
"If you find the reign of God, you don't need anything else;
it relativizes all other treasures."

11. THE REIGN OF GOD 2 60
"The living tradition alone passes on the full Christian life."

12. THE SOWER 64
"Where are you?"

13. THE WIDOW AND THE UNJUST JUDGE 69
"Will not God in his goodness provide
the help that you need if you keep asking?"

14. THE WORKMEN IN THE VINEYARD 74
"The invitation of grace to enter the kingdom goes forth
again and again and again."

15. THE HIDDEN TREASURE 81
"The treasure of eternal life is given without our seeking it.
It is already there."

PART III. GOD KNOWS NO BOUNDARIES

16. THE GOOD SAMARITAN 90
"The kingdom of God is open to everyone."

17. THE PRODIGAL SON 2 99
"You are always with me. Everything I have is yours."

18. LAZARUS AND THE RICH MAN 107
"God does not set up barriers. We do."

19. THE GREAT DINNER 115
"God comes to those who consent to come to God
with their lives just as they are."

20. THE NEW WINE 121
"The exuberance of the Spirit cannot be contained
in the old structures."

EPILOGUE: 127
The Coming of the Kingdom

PUBLISHER'S NOTE

SOME YEARS AGO, FR. THOMAS KEATING published *The Kingdom of God Is Like...,* a collection of reflections and homilies he had offered to various communities, including especially the community at St. Benedict's Monastery in Snowmass, Colorado. While the title of that collection pointed to the parables that comprised the majority of the book, the book also included other material not related to parables, such as a reflection on the rich young man (Mark 10:17–27) who is invited by Jesus to give his money to the poor.

Since earlier Fr. Keating books, such as *Awakenings* and *Reawakenings,* also include some chapters devoted to various parables, readers over the years have asked if Crossroad would gather together in a single volume his meditations on the parables of Jesus. This present volume meets that need. The content, drawn from those three books, appears here virtually unchanged, grouped together according to three central themes. We hope that this book will be of interest both to readers already familiar with Fr. Keating's writing and those who, discovering Fr. Keating for the first time, seek a trustworthy guide for reflecting on these timeless and always surprising and challenging words of Jesus.

FOREWORD

ABOUT A YEAR AFTER THE PUBLICATION of my *Hear Then the Parable,* I received a letter from a young minister in Northern Ireland involved in the peace movement, surely one of the most frustrating ministries around. He wrote that my analysis of the parable of the withered fig tree had spoken to his soul for it so accurately described his situation—he just keeps on manuring, hoping that somehow God will give life.

I wrote back thanking him for the letter, but saying that the credit should go to the parable teller, not the parable critic. The parable, not my exegesis, spoke to his soul. This is not some false humility, for I remember clearly the night I first worked up that section of the book. The parable did not impress me, since I thought it a minor one compared to some of the other ones. Furthermore, I was under some pressure to finish the chapter. I thought I knew Jesus' style and techniques as parable teller. As I mulled over the parable, I was struck by the futility of the man's effort, by the use of the term "manure" (actually more accurately "dung"), and by the ellipsis, which most translators fill in: "If it bears fruit, well…," and a shrug of the shoulders. Not much I thought, but typical of Jesus. More typical than I thought, because the stone the builder rejected has become the cornerstone. I'm delighted that Father Keating sees in this parable a symbol of the contemplative life.

Father Keating's *Meditations on the Parables of Jesus* is itself elliptical like the parables. His sermons leave unsaid what should not be spoken and to the hearer the story's remainder. His style of preaching is immensely faithful to the parables, for he does not tell, but listens and joins his audience as co-hearers of the parables. Over and over again, he responds to the parable story with a story, each time leaving us to hear again. Or as Jesus challenged, "the one who has ears, had better hear."

Father Keating has four sermons on the parable of the leaven, one of the shortest and one might think least significant parables in the tradition, one on which even the evangelists do not comment. He seizes on the parable's radical nature, its unmasking of monumental evil. The parable is a lens on the everyday, exposing the presence of God where we dare not expect it, where we have been trained to ignore it. He sees miracle where it truly is. Not just in a mother's forgiveness of and caring for her son's murderer, but more importantly in the barely perceptible tear in the eye of the sociopath. For him the kingdom is not the bloom of a barren fig tree, but God's touch is enough.

By turning the parables over and over, Keating allows them to refocus the nonparabolic elements of the Jesus tradition. One might think that Jesus as King would be contrary to the monumental evil, the everydayness of the parables. But Keating shows they are of one piece, that Jesus's abandonment in death is the monumental evil and his resurrection is the mask that hides that abandonment, but exposes the miracle of God's great love.

We are perhaps too accustomed to think of the parables as simple stories for simple people. Such an attitude only cloaks our own arrogance. Keating restores Jesus as the artist of the soul, and he responds as an artist. One can only be astounded at how these parables continue to generate insights into the most profound issues of life.

—**Bernard Brandon Scott**
Darbeth Distinguished Professor
of New Testament
Phillips Graduate Seminary,
Tulsa, Oklahoma

AUTHOR'S PREFACE

THIS THIRD VOLUME OF HOMILIES, following *Awakenings* and *Reawakenings,* owes much of its inspiration to the scholarly and insightful book by Bernard Brandon Scott, *Hear Then the Parable.* The scripture texts given at the beginning of each chapter omit the settings and conclusions of the parables, which many exegetes believe to be the work of the evangelists themselves. (See Funk, Scott, and Butts, *The Parables of Jesus: Red Letter Edition.*)

The laborious work of Scott and other scholars in seeking the original meaning of the parables brings into sharp focus aspects of Jesus' teaching and personality that have not been previously emphasized. When rightly understood, the parables help us to see how extraordinary a wisdom teacher Jesus really was, and how revolutionary, in the best sense of that word, was the content of what he taught and to which he bore witness by his life and death.

These insights cohere particularly well with the actual experience of people on the spiritual journey. When contemplative prayer is seriously embraced, we come upon the lived reality that Scott details so well: the reversal of expectations, the gradual and often painful liberation from emotional programs for happiness, and the increasing discovery of the kingdom of God in the ordinary and in the everyday. So often the experience of "corruption"—that which is first looked upon as crisis or catastrophe—is actually the occasion of the inbreaking of the kingdom, as God invites us to change not so much the situation as our attitudes.

I am grateful to Bernard Brandon Scott for allowing me to publish his ideas in popular form and to share the significant implications that I find in them for the following of Christ. And I am grateful to the first hearers of these homilies—the monks and the extended community at St. Benedict's Monastery, Snowmass, Colorado, and the many participants at Contemplative Outreach Intensive Retreats, where these ideas have first been aired and evaluated.

GOD DWELLS IN
THE ORDINARY

THE PUBLICAN AND THE PHARISEE

"Two people went up to the temple *to pray, one a Pharisee and the other a tax collector. The Pharisee, standing by himself, was praying thus, 'God, I thank you that I am not like other people: thieves, rogues, adulterers, or even like this tax collector. I fast twice a week; I give a tenth of all my income.' But the tax collector, standing far off, would not even look up to heaven, but was beating his breast and saying, 'God, be merciful to me, a sinner!' I tell you, this man went down to his home justified rather than the other." (Luke 18:10–14a)*

The parable of the publican and the Pharisee reinforces one of the central themes of the parable of the good Samaritan. The coming of the good Samaritan down the road to Jericho signals the end of the social landscape and map of the kingdom of God as perceived by Jesus' contemporaries. This point is somewhat obscured by the manner in which Luke introduces and concludes this parable in his gospel.

He predisposes the reader to look upon the Pharisee as prideful. In fact, the Pharisee only did what the temple map required of those who were considered insiders and members of the religious elite of the time. In fact, the social context of the temple, as we now know it from other historical documents, would depict him as the ideal pious Pharisee! His speech is repeated almost word for word in other examples we have of pious prayers from the same period. His conduct and prayers are typical of the devout Pharisee.

The same map determining the proper conduct of one belonging to the sacred precincts of the temple as an insider also determines the place, the stance, and prayer of the publican (tax collector). He belongs to the group outside the bounds of the temple. He stands apart because he knows such is his proper place as an outsider. The place that he took was not a manifestation of his humility, as Luke hints, but simply of his awareness of his proper place as a sinner.

Thus the two men described in the parable manifest their relative places and status in the accepted culture of the time. One belongs to the sacred precincts of the temple and is an insider. The other belongs to the secular world and is an outsider. The social map calls for him to pray apart from the Pharisee who represents the holy. Thus from the text there is no evidence of merit or blame in the conduct or prayers of the two men.

✣ *The sacred has moved to everyday life.* The storyteller stuns the hearers with his conclusion: "The publican went home to his house (to the secular world) justified. The other man did not." These words come like a peal of thunder to the crowd. Luke attributes this statement to the humility of the publican and to the pride of the Pharisee, but the publican did not even make restitution for his extortions as Zacchaeus did (Luke 19:1–9) and the Pharisee thanked God for his good deeds, as was customary in the prayers of a devout Pharisee of his time.

Thus the main point of the parable emerges with stark clarity. The social map of the time is being abandoned and the kingdom of God is no longer to be found in the temple. The holy is outside and the unholy may be inside. The activity of the kingdom of God has moved from the sacred precincts of the temple to the profane arena of the secular world. The Pharisee represents well the piety of the temple. The publican represents well the secular world. The sacred place is no longer the place of the sacred. The sacred has moved to everyday life.

THE MUSTARD SEED

"WHAT IS THE KINGDOM OF GOD LIKE? And to what shall I compare it? It is like a mustard seed that someone took and sowed in the garden; it grew and became a tree, and the birds of the air made nests in its branches." (Luke 13:18–19)

The thrust of the parables is to subvert the distorted myths in which people live their lives. To understand what we mean by "living in a myth" just think of a couple of our own contemporary myths. Take the myth of "the All American Boy," for example. This is the young man who gets straight A's in college and graduate school, climbs the executive ladder, and perhaps becomes the head of a multinational. Or the "American Dream:" two cars in every garage, vacations in Florida, houses in Spain, and so forth. On a more serious level, the American dream has been a

vision of America's invincibility, of its absolute enti-
tlement in the eyes of God.

A myth is often what holds people's lives together. It
is an attempt to resolve the tensions of everyday life
by promising an idealized future in which one will be
rescued from all the problems of ordinary life. When
a myth begins to falter, great leaders may try to find
ways to recapture the glory of earlier days, like John
F. Kennedy's effort to rekindle the American dream
by sending a man to the moon. American astronauts
did go to the moon, but meanwhile the Vietnam war
devastated the prestige of American invincibility and
with it the American dream.

For the Israelites of Jesus' time, the tension between
everyday reality and a mythical vision of Israel as God's
chosen people was felt with particular urgency. From
the heyday of national power and prestige during
the reigns of King David and King Solomon, Israel
had been on a downhill slide for several centuries, its
kingdom conquered and divided several times over.
If one lives in occupied territories, as the Israelites of
Jesus' time did, the question naturally arises, "Is this
ghastly oppression by the Romans a punishment from
God, or is our suffering just part of the human condition?" In the particular myth in which the people of
first-century Israel were living, the kingdom of God
had specific connotations of power, triumph, holiness,

and goodness. The kingdom, when it came, would introduce a glorious new age of universal peace, with God's chosen people at the head of the nations.

The cultural symbol for this myth was the great cedar of Lebanon. Cedars of Lebanon were comparable to the huge redwood trees of California. They grew straight up for two or three hundred feet or more. Every kind of bird could enjoy their shade. This image was deeply embedded in the cultural conditioning of the Jewish people. The kingdom of God as a nation would be the greatest of all nations just as the great cedar of Lebanon was the greatest of all trees.

Instead, Jesus proposed this parable, "What is the kingdom of God really like? It is like a mustard seed"—proverbially the smallest and most insignificant of all seeds—"that someone took and sowed in his garden." For an alert hearer of Jesus' day, the detail about the garden would be a tip-off. In the Jewish view of the world, order was identified with holiness and disorder with uncleanness. Hence there were very strict rules about what could be planted in a household garden. The rabbinical law of diverse kinds ruled that one could not mix certain plants in the same garden. A mustard plant was forbidden in a household garden because it was fast spreading and would tend to invade the veggies. In stating that this man planted a mustard seed in his garden, the hearers are alerted to the fact that he was doing something illegal. An unclean image thus becomes the starting point for Jesus' vision of the kingdom of God in this parable.

✢ *We do not have to wait for an apocalyptic deliverance. The kingdom is available right now.*

If the starting point is an unclean image, the rest of the parable becomes even more perplexing. What do we know about a mustard seed, botanically speaking? It is a common, fast-spreading plant, which grows to about four feet in height. It puts out a few branches, and with some stretch of the imagination, birds might build a few down-at-the-heel nests in its shade.

Steeped in their cultural images of the great cedar of Lebanon, the hearers would be expecting the mustard seed, Jesus' symbol of the kingdom, to grow into a mighty apocalyptic tree. Jesus' point is exactly the opposite. It just becomes a bush. Thus the image of the kingdom of God as a towering cedar of Lebanon is explicitly ridiculed. According to Jesus, the kingdom of God is like a mustard seed, which some man illegally planted in his garden. It became a shrub and a few birds nested in its modest branches. That's all. The parable subverts all the grandiose ideas about what the kingdom is going to be like when it finally arrives.

8

One of the most firmly held Israelite expectations was that the kingdom of God would manifest the final triumph of God in history. Its arrival, heralded by the long-awaited Messiah, would rescue Israel from its miserable subservience to the Roman Empire. It was a future kingdom, not one in the here-and-now. Jesus' parable implies that if we accept the God of everyday life, we can find God in everyday life. We do not have to wait for an apocalyptic deliverance. We do not have to wait for a grandiose liberation. The kingdom is available right now.

✠

The parables, according to Scott, are like handles on the mystery of the kingdom, pointers suggesting both what it is and what it is not. We cannot fully understand the kingdom because it is a mystery that transcends any possibility of being contained in a concept. But by rotating the wisdom of Jesus' sayings in our mind's eye and with the help of the parables, we can at least get a glimpse of it.

A parable points to something we only gradually come to know as we absorb the teaching of Jesus. In this parable he intimates that God is not necessarily going to intervene in this world for the triumph of the just. He may not intervene in an apocalyptic manner to deliver Israel or bring about justice and peace. He has entrusted the latter to us. We are not to wait around for an apocalyptic intervention to do the job.

If we lead a holy life—as opposed to a merely respectable one—we are likely to lose most of our friends and relatives. We might get one or two of them to follow our example, but it is like the mustard seed. We may get a modest result, but it is not in the nature of a cedar of Lebanon. All we are likely to get is an inconspicuous shrub of which there are plenty of others all around in great variety. The mustard seed is just one step ahead of being an ordinary weed.

How are we to understand this deliberate use by Jesus of the unclean and insignificant as images of his kingdom? It suggests that God's greatest works are not done on a grandiose level. Not in cathedrals, big buildings, or large mausoleums. Cathedrals can become museums rather than sources of inspiration for the Christian community. The kingdom is in everyday life with its ups and downs, and above all, in its insignificance. Such is where most people actually live their lives. The kingdom is thus readily accessible to everybody.

The parable affirms that grace is like a mustard seed sown in us, the smallest of all seeds. It is growing, but it is not going to turn us into a cedar of Lebanon. We will be doing well if we become modest shrubs.

So hard was it for people of Jesus' time to get over their idea of the kingdom of God as a triumphant institution that even the

✤ Grace is like a mustard seed sown in us, the smallest of all seeds.

evangelists tried to change it into something great anyway. In other words, the myth recaptured the parable. The parable was meant to change one's idea about the kingdom, but what happened was that the old mindset began to interpret the parable in a way that was consistent with its former mythical expectations. There are four versions of this parable in the Gospels, three in the synoptics and one in the Gospel of Thomas, a document recovered about fifty years ago in the Nag Hammadi Gnostic Collection, which many exegetes think is closer in some places to the original oral tradition. For Luke and Matthew, contrary to all botanical good sense, the mustard seed does turn into a tree. In Mark, it turns into the greatest of shrubs. In Thomas, it turns into a great branch so that a lot of birds can rest in its shade. All of these expectations are contrary to the facts. A mustard seed does not become a tree, the greatest of shrubs, or put forth a great branch, however much one may want it to. The oral tradition was evidently influenced by the old expectations of grandeur as people gradually slipped back into their former mindsets. They lost the radical thrust and the incredible freedom to which the parable called them. For us too, it is a threat to our preconceived ideas and mythical belief systems, and hence there is a strong tendency to resist its stark realism.

⊕

If we are looking for a great expansion of our particular religion, nation, ethnic group, social movement, or whatever, into some great visible organization that fills the earth, we are on the wrong track. This is not God's idea of success. Where are the mightiest works of the kingdom accomplished? In our attitudes and hence in secret. Where there is charity, there is God. Opportunities to work for the homeless, the starving, the aging, are all readily available. No one may notice our good deeds, including ourselves. The kingdom of God manifests itself in the modest changes in our attitudes and in the little improvements in our behavior that no one may notice, including ourselves. These are the mighty works of God, not great external accomplishments.

"To what shall I liken the kingdom of God?" Jesus asked. The kingdom is manifested in ordinary daily life and how we live it. Can we accept the God of everyday life? If we can, then we can enjoy the kingdom here and now, without having to wait for an apocalypse or someone to deliver us from our difficulties.

THE LOST COIN

"WHAT WOMAN HAVING TEN SILVER COINS, *if she loses one of them, does not light a lamp, and search carefully until she finds it? When she has found it, she calls together her friends and neighbors, saying, 'Rejoice with me, for I have found the coin that I had lost.'"* (Luke 15:8–9)

This parable is not unlike the parable of the mustard seed. In that parable, as we saw, the Lord seems to be burlesquing the popular expectations of the kingdom as a giant cedar of Lebanon. As if Jesus were to say, "You are looking for a cedar of Lebanon, the great apocalyptic tree, and all I am asking of you is to become an insignificant little shrub."

If we can imagine the astonished faces of the hearers, it is not hard to picture Jesus' amusement at the collapsing of their house of cards. This parable continues in a similar vein.

A certain woman has lost a coin. A drachma was about the same as a denarius, one day's wage for a common laborer. It was not a lot of money. But she is looking everywhere for this coin, sweeping the house up and down. Some of the hearers are now getting excited and want to help her. When she finally finds it, there is great joy! She calls friends and neighbors, and they rejoice over her recovery of the tiny sum.

Jesus once again juxtaposes the grandiose expectations in the popular mind regarding how the kingdom is expected to appear in our lives, and how it actually appears. The woman finally finds the coin of modest value. That is the extent of God's intervention. Thus the kingdom is identified with the ordinary. She did not win the state lottery. Jesus undermines grandiose expectations of all kinds . For one reason: they are not likely to happen.

In the three parables that appear in chapter fifteen of Luke—the prodigal son, the lost sheep, and the lost coin—Luke seems to be intent on justifying Jesus' conduct in eating and drinking with public sinners. In his view, Jesus' purpose is to call them to repentance. In fact, the original meaning of the texts according to contemporary exegetes has little to do with repentance but focuses rather on the nature of the kingdom.

✣

In the Gospel of Thomas a number of the parables are found in a different form from that reported in the synoptic Gospels. There is one parable that appears only in Thomas. Many exegetes think it is genuine because it follows the patterns that are familiar in Jesus' parables: shock value, an undermining of grandiose ideas about the kingdom, and identification of the kingdom with the unclean, the marginalized, and the outcasts of society.

The parable reminds us of the story of the widow of Zarephath in 1 Kings 17:8–15. There was a great famine in her country. The prophet Elijah, in desperate hunger, asked the widow for a morsel of bread and she replied that she had nothing to give him. The prophet then miraculously filled her empty jar saying, "The jar of meal shall not be spent, nor the cruze of oil, until the day that the Lord sends rain upon the earth."

The parable in the Gospel of Thomas has a different ending:

THE KINGDOM OF GOD *is like a certain woman who was carrying a jar full of meal. While she was walking on a road still some distance from home, the handle of the jar broke and the meal emptied out behind her on the road. She did not realize it. She had noticed no accident. When she reached her house she set the jar down and found it was empty.* (Thomas 97)

✥ *There is no place to go to find the kingdom because it is always close at hand.*

This story tells us that the kingdom of God is present in failure, accident, and emptiness. In her case, there was no prophet to come to her rescue, no visible divine intervention. There was just accident, failure, everydayness, the ordinary. The teaching of Jesus is that those are precisely the situations where the miraculous activity of the kingdom takes place. This means that the kingdom must be active at a deeper level than we are normally looking for or expecting. Nowhere does Jesus say there is *no* divine intervention. It is just not on the level that we would like it to be. In this remarkable parable, the divine intervention is represented by the empty jar.

This raises the question, "Is God just as present in absence as in presence?" Or to put it another way, "Is the divine intervention always there supporting us whether we think it is present or not?"

The answer of the parables is emphatically yes. The kingdom of God is active in failure, ordinariness, everydayness. If we wait for a miraculous rescue, a vindictive triumph, or for some idealized lifestyle to appear, we are looking for the wrong kingdom, certainly not the one that Jesus is revealing.

✤

There is no place to go to find the kingdom because it is always close at hand. We do not need to look for success because the kingdom is equally present in failure. What is disconcerting for the hearers in both of these parables is that the kingdom is not only present and active in failure and in ordinariness, but is at work in the unclean, in the prostitutes and tax collectors to whom Jesus extends table fellowship.

According to Jesus, God is in total solidarity with ordinary daily life with its poignant failures in the spiritual journey as well as in everything else. Thus God's mercy invites us to show compassion and solidarity with all the other sinners in the world, including public sinners and street people, who in the parable of the great dinner, are the only ones who finally got in (Luke 14:16–24).

The kingdom is present not in grandiose accomplishments, but in showing practical love in humble ways, day after day, and in refusing to allow our failures and disappointments to hide God's love from us. God invites us to share the divine emptiness. The divine emptiness might also be described as total vulnerability: the willingness to be hurt over and over again without loving less but more. That means never giving up on anyone, not even on ourselves. Of such is the kingdom of God.

Four

THE LEAVEN 1

"**The kingdom of God is like yeast** *that a woman took and mixed in with three measures of flour until all of it was leavened." (Matthew 13:33)*

If the kingdom of God is like leaven, Jesus' teaching is absolutely revolutionary. In the ancient Israelite world, leaven—today's yeast—was a symbol of corruption. Modern English usage has given it a positive sense—fermentation and new life. But for the people of Israel, leaven was the archetype of corruption. It symbolized the unholy, the profane, everyday life. *Un*leavened bread was the proper symbol of the holy, the sacred, the feast. Why was leaven regarded as such a lively symbol of corruption? In ancient times leaven was made by placing a piece of bread in a dark, damp place until it rotted and stank.

In Jesus' one-sentence tale, a woman took leaven and put it in three measures of flour, an amount sufficient to feed about fifty people. This is the exact measurement that we hear about in other places in scripture.

✥ *Look for the kingdom in the most unexpected places.* Abraham ordered his wife Sarah to make three measures of bread for his three angelic visitors at the Oaks of Mamre. Hannah made this offering when she presented Samuel in the temple. The amount is thus related to epiphanies of God in the Old Testament. But the epiphany here is quite different; it is an epiphany of corruption. In this case, the leaven is kneaded into an enormous amount of dough and in due time the whole batch becomes leavened. Are we to understand that the kingdom of God is working like leaven in the dough to form a huge mass of corruption?

The hearers are naturally asking the question, "Is this man saying that good is evil?" Jesus' parables work not only through similarities, but, as Scott points out, through dissimilarities. The usual image of leaven as the symbol of corruption is used in this parable to emphasize the negative aspect—or what seems like the negative aspect—of the kingdom. For one thing, the parable questions the hearers' easy assumption of the predictability of what is good and what is evil. It confronts their preconceptions regarding where goodness is to be found. In this respect, it coheres with the parable of the good Samaritan where, as we will see, the boundaries of social stratification are dramatically subverted. The Samaritan, the Israelite's epitome of the bad guy, turns out to be a hero.

In this parable, an even more profound boundary is being challenged. Can evil be good? Recalling Jesus' custom of reaching out in table fellowship with the outcasts of society, the kingdom of God is revealed to be active in marginal people and in the marginalized. Where is the kingdom if it is not in the holy, the sacred, and the acceptable places? Jesus, by his example and preaching, says, "Look for it in the most unexpected places." According to the parables, the kingdom of God is free to appear anywhere, any time, and under any guise. It does not fit into our presuppositions or expectations, and still less, our demands. In fact, it deliberately removes, prop by prop, everything holding up our ideas of the nature of the kingdom and where it is to be found.

✠

A story might help to grasp the shock value of this saying. An acquaintance of mine in California with a very active and ongoing practice of contemplative prayer, experienced terrible tragedy. Her only son, a young man just coming out of college with every promise for

21

a brilliant future, was shot to death on the street for no reason at all by a sociopath, a man who just wanted to kill somebody for the sheer pleasure of exercising absolute power over someone. The murderer was convicted and sent to prison. Of course, the mother was devastated by the senseless murder of her son. She was plagued by the harrowing questions: "Why couldn't God have done something to prevent it? Why did it have to be my son? Is this a punishment for my sins? Does God really love me?" For her, the tragedy was unmitigated evil, monumental corruption.

After much prayer she decided to write this man and tell him that she forgave him. For a year she received no response. Finally a very matter-of-fact letter came, acknowledging her letter but without the least sign of remorse. She wrote back asking if he would be willing to see her. Again a wait of about a year. Finally a note came saying yes. She drove the long distance to the prison, and accompanied by the social worker assigned to his case, she met the murderer of her son. He spent most of the time describing, absolutely deadpan, the horrendous childhood he had suffered. He was an unwanted child, continually subjected to physical abuse in the extreme. As a consequence, he had become totally antisocial and narcissistic. At one point in the conversation, he confessed, "You cannot imagine the immense joy I felt when I stood over your son and realized that I had killed him!" It was his moment of ultimate power. For the first time the sense of self-worth that had been systematically crushed by his whole previous life experience flooded over him to the point of ecstatic triumph.

The mother stood her ground. Her forgiveness was unshaken, and she reaffirmed it to him. The social worker was flabbergasted by the spirit of this woman who could calmly forgive the one who had caused her the greatest pain of her life. The social worker wrote to her sometime later saying, "This man has started to change. He shows a little more courtesy and consideration for the other inmates."

The woman felt moved to stay in contact with the prisoner. She offered to return. His immediate response was poignant: "Please don't come again. I'm afraid, if you keep coming, I'll have to face the unbearable pain of my childhood." His antisocial behavior had enabled him to maintain absolute denial of a past that was too painful to face up to. But she did go back. At the end of the interview, she embraced him.

I do not know what the final outcome of this exchange will be. She is still writing, still visiting him, still feeling the pain of her great loss. In her last interview, she detected as she gave him a farewell hug, a tiny tear in the corner of his eye. In a very real sense, she has become his mother and he is becoming her son.

✦

Was God's kingdom active in the monumental corruption involved in this event? Perhaps the movement of one person from total inhumanity to the capacity to shed a single tear is a greater act of God than the sanctification of a saint? Who can judge? Jesus often identified himself with the outcasts of society that everybody had given up on by sharing a meal with them. Evidently the kingdom of God was active there. The kingdom, of course, is at work everywhere, but the parable suggests that it is mightiest in the marginalized and in events that we characterize as unmitigated evil. To draw a single tear, to us almost imperceptible, from a heart of stone must cause all creation to vibrate with joy and wonder at the power of the kingdom and of God's love.

Five

THE LEAVEN 2

"THE KINGDOM OF GOD IS LIKE YEAST *which a woman took and mixed in with three measures of flour until all of it was leavened." (Matthew 13:33)*

Jesus says the kingdom of God is like leaven. In the ancient Mediterranean world, as we saw, leaven had very negative associations. It was the archetype of uncleanness and corruption. Leaven was made by putting a piece of bread in a dark, damp place until it molded and stank. Both leaven and the process of leavening were symbols of corruption.

In the Jewish tradition men were considered ritually pure and women were ritually unclean. As a consequence, rabbis were forbidden to speak to women in public. No rabbi giving a formal sermon would cite a woman as heroine of any story. Jesus frequently did so in his parables, however, ignoring the stereotypes of his day.

In this parable Jesus addresses the popular idea that the kingdom of God is holy, good, and triumphant. The kingdom turns out to be active in the marginalized and the poor, both of whom were regarded in Jesus' day as objects of God's abandonment. The state of poverty was regarded as the result of sin and hence was a symbol of corruption. Natural calamities were also regarded as punishments from God.

In this parable a woman takes leaven, the archetype of corruption, and hides it in three measures of flour, the same amount that Sarah used to make bread for the angels who visited Abraham at Mamre. There is thus the implication in the parable of a divine epiphany. Moreover, the enormous amount of dough that is leavened suggests not just ordinary corruption, but monumental corruption.

The hearers are surely thinking, "How can the kingdom of God, which is supposed to be holy, good, and triumphant, be like leaven, the archetype of corruption? Is the preacher implying that evil is good?"

✜

Let me propose a story that seems to raise the same issues as this parable. The great popular art form of our time is the movies. Once in a while one of them proposes similar questions to those that arise in the parables. Some years ago I saw a movie called *Our Sons*. It was about two mothers, with two gay sons. One of the mothers was a poor woman whose fundamentalist religious background caused her to regard her son's lifestyle as an absolute taboo; she had completely dis-associated herself from him. The other woman was upper middle-class and a well-to-do liberal. She con-sidered herself to have adjusted well to the situation. In fact, she was just as angry and resentful as the other mother, but in her own way. It was clear to her son that he was not accepted.

As the plot unfolds, the son of the poor woman is dying of AIDS and longs to see his mother once again, but is afraid to write to her. His friend per-suades his own mother, as a special favor to him, to visit the poor woman and pay for her to travel to see her dying son. The poor mother turns out to be a down-to-earth woman who sees through the denial of the other mother. *Our Sons* might have been called "our growth." A growth process is clearly taking place in the two mothers as they struggle with their common humiliation. The behavior of the sons is an equal no-no for both of them, though each reacts in a different way.

Finally, when the poor woman comes to see her dying son, she makes several visits but each time she stays

✥ *The kingdom of God manifests itself in solidarity with other people, in sympathy with their misfortune, and in unconditional love.* near the door. Something inside her remains fearful and unreconciled. The son is getting weaker and weaker as death approaches. When it is time for her to return to her home, she comes for a final visit and to say good-bye. This time she cautiously tiptoes over to his bed. The camera focuses on her hand as she ever-so-slowly and cautiously reaches out and touches her son's hand extended toward her. She has at last overcome her prejudices and fears.

✥

The kingdom of God is active where we perceive monumental corruption. If the poor mother had not reached out and touched her son in a sign of recon-ciliation and forgiveness, what would have become of her? She would have remained permanently walled up in her own security system, desperately trying to protect herself from the pain of the reality of the situ-ation and from the demands of true love.

The divine action makes use of what seems like cor-ruption in our eyes to change us, to open us to the kingdom, which is present where we least expect it. The kingdom of God is present and available in what happens. The question is not why upsetting or devastating things happen, but what we are going to do with them now that they are happening? The divine compassion is intervening in our behalf, but not on the level we want it to be or can perceive it to be. It is working mightily at a deeper level where grace enables us to say yes to God in the events of daily life.

In reaching out to her son, the mother opened herself to God's salvation. By being reconciled with her son, she enabled him to die in peace. The kingdom of God manifests itself in solidarity with other people, in sympathy with their misfortune, and in unconditional love. It is most active in situations that seem to us to represent monumental corruption.

The Jewish religion of the time identified everyday life with corruption and the sacred with the temple rituals and the great feasts. Jesus teaches that everyday life is the place of the sacred. The temple is no longer the place to look for it. Everyday life is the arena where the kingdom is most powerful. The kingdom is especially present and active when we are confronting what we think is monumental corruption. What are we to do with it? Jesus does not give the answer in the parable; he just invites us to beware of predicting, on the basis of our prepackaged beliefs, what is good and what is evil.

Six

THE LEAVEN 3

"THE KINGDOM OF GOD IS LIKE YEAST *that a woman took and mixed in with three measures of flour until all of it was leavened." (Matthew 13:33)*

How can the kingdom be like leaven? The teaching of Jesus challenges our attempts to discern what is good or evil on the basis of the accepted norms of the sacred in our respective cultures. In the Israelite society, leavened bread represented the unholy, the everyday, while unleavened bread represented the sacred, the feast day. Jesus implies that the kingdom of God may appear under any guise including corruption. Thus Jesus ate with outcasts, sinners, and the marginalized. In fact, he ate more meals with them than with the religious authorities of his time. By sitting down to table with sinners, which in his culture was a statement of identification with their community, Jesus forfeited his own moral purity.

Did that significant gesture mean that he approved of extortion, prostitution, and the various forms of misbehavior of public sinners? Obviously his table

✠ A difficult situation can be a great blessing, an opportunity for God to heal us at the deepest level.

fellowship with them did not mean approval of sinful behavior. What his conduct did reveal was that reaching out in love, reconciliation, and forgiveness are vastly more important in God's eyes than moral incorruption.

What forms might monumental corruption take for us today? It could be an accident resulting in a serious physical or mental disability. It could be what we regard as moral reprobation in someone dear to us, as in the case of the two sons in the previous chapter, or it could be a problem in our own conscience. In the eyes of the beholder the situation looks like a disaster. In reality, it can be a great blessing, an opportunity for God to heal us at the deepest level.

✠

An extraordinary example of monumental corruption of a physical kind is exemplified for me in the life of the daughter of one of our neighbors. This child was injured early in life and for the past twenty-two years has been completely helpless, requiring twenty-four hour a day care on the part of her parents. She cannot feed, dress, or do anything for herself. She just is. These parents have shown this child so much love and caring that she seems to enjoy a sense of complete security. When you look into the eyes of this girl, you have the sense of looking into the eyes of someone who has no fear; of one who because of the heroic devotion of her parents, has been able to remain a child all her life retaining all the delightful qualities of childhood. She cannot walk, speak, or move her body; but she looks at you with utter simplicity, and the depth of acceptance in her eyes is like looking into the eyes of God. The acceptance of the tragedy and their response to it has enabled her parents to connect with God's love in an extraordinary way.

In the light of this example, I venture to suggest that our attitude toward what we regard as monumental corruption has to be changed, not the corrupting situation itself. Our tendency of course is to want to change the painful or shameful situation right away. But some situations are designed to change us, and our acceptance of them marks the place where our personal redemption really begins

✠

This parable of the leaven sounds the same chord that will later reverberate fully in Jesus' own personal experience of monumental corruption. When God's Son dies on the cross, not a single angel or human comes to his aid. The Father of this Son, as far as external evidence goes, could not care less about what happens to him. Jesus is rejected by the civil and religious ✣ *Some situations are designed to change us.* authorities and by his own people, and abandoned by his disciples. From the cross he witnesses his life and teaching destroyed before his eyes.

Our experience of abandonment, the seeming absence of God on the spiritual journey, together with our temptations and the tendency to moral failure that frightens us, may actually be a powerful manifestation of the kingdom, according to the extraordinary reversal of values that Jesus proposes as the path to perfect joy and freedom.

Few people have understood this teaching. Saint Francis of Assisi was one. There is a story in which a favorite disciple, Brother Leo, asks him what perfect happiness is. Saint Francis answers, "Suppose you arrive cold and hungry at the gate of a monastery on a snowy night, and the porter slams the door in your face. Standing in the snow, shivering, you plead for mercy. He comes out and beats you with a stick. Ah! Brother Leo, that is perfect happiness!"

The kingdom of God does not operate on the level of appearances, and rarely on the level of signs and wonders, but God's apparent absence in daily life does not mean that the divine intervention is not present. On the contrary, it is present in a very real but hidden way. The kingdom manifests its incomparable power by changing our inner dispositions and attitudes. There may be no great deliverance, no sensational conversion; just small changes for the better in the way we react to the same old routines and our customary failures.

God is not limited by our ideas of where the kingdom may or may not be functioning. As we saw in the parable of the Pharisee and the publican, it is clearly not limited to sacred places. It is focused in everyday life. More precisely, it is present in the apparent corrupting situations of everyday life. Indeed, the parable implies that the power of the kingdom is more active there than anywhere else.

God reserves the right to appear under any guise. But because our self-centeredness is so deeply ingrained, it may take monumental corruption of some kind for us to begin to question our attitudes and motivation. These are what have to be changed, not necessarily the situation.

Who is this God whose chief command is that we forgive and show love for one another? If God loves us infinitely, God must be totally involved in our moral melodrama. We believe, in fact, that God has taken upon and into Godself in the person of Jesus Christ, all our sinfulness—that is, our whole experience of monumental corruption in ourselves and its consequences in our lives. In other words, God expects us to go on trusting God implicitly even in the face of our own monumental moral corruption. In a poem by Thomas Merton, the question is raised, "Who is God?" The response is, "Mercy, within mercy, within mercy."

Seven

THE LEAVEN 4

"THE KINGDOM OF GOD IS LIKE YEAST
*which a woman took and mixed in with three measures of
flour until all of it was leavened." (Matthew 13:33)*

It is characteristic of the parables to ask the question,
"What makes you think that the world is the way you
see it?"

In the minds of the Jewish hearers of the time, the
kingdom of God had certain connotations suggesting the ultimate triumph of God in the world. The
kingdom as Jesus sees it turns out to be quite different.
The life and death of Jesus, in which God does not
intervene, indicates that the kingdom of God is not
to be found in miraculous occurrences, in being rescued from the inevitable results of our stupidity and
misdeeds, in having all our needs amply provided for,

or even in overcoming our sins, but rather in living our lives in union with God.

According to the parables, God is in complete solidarity with the outcasts of society. Escape into an ideal kind of lifestyle or rescue from life's difficulties and problems are both rejected by Jesus as solutions to the problems of living in this world. The solution is not in getting away from our problems, but in realizing that God is totally present and supporting us in them. The most striking example of this is that God does not destroy death, but joins us in death. Our expectations of becoming paragons of piety, great contemplatives, attaining higher stages of consciousness—all subtly aimed at carrying us beyond the daily troubles of ordinary life—are not the way into the kingdom. Rather, the kingdom consists in finding God *in* our disappointments, failures, problems, and even in our inability to rid ourselves of our vices.

⚜

I joined the Trappists in 1944, long before the reforms of the Second Vatican Council. After having lived a strict monastic life for six years, in which I followed all the rules, appeared at all the spiritual exercises, never overslept or overate, wore the religious habit all the time including to bed, tried not to judge those who did not keep the rule as well as I did, rarely spoke to anybody except the abbot and novice master, worked hard, wrote home only once or twice a year, rarely had a visit from relatives and friends—in short, after I had faithfully practiced all the austerities of the Trappist Order, the monastery burned down. I was breathing smoke as I came down the stairway from the dormitory to the guesthouse—there was no other means of escape—into the source of the fire. The building was a fire trap from the word go. If it had not been for someone calling, "Stay close to the floor and come this way," I would have died of smoke inhalation. I leapt out a first-floor window and landed in a snowbank. It was then that the insight came to me: "Maybe God isn't as interested in this highly structured lifestyle as I am!"

It took another twenty years to work that insight into my monastic vision. It is hard for any insight to penetrate a mindset that is profoundly culturally conditioned, which is certainly the case in any form of strict religious training. It may take disappointment, tragedy, illness, loss of friends, and near death experiences to shake us free.

The parables perform a similar service. They suggest that our idea of the kingdom may not be the correct one. Our ideas of God and the kingdom need to be expanded and to grow continuously. God is just as present in human relationships and in nature as in religious services. While religious rituals certainly have significant value, they are not to be identified with the kingdom. For the kingdom of God is in internal attitudes rather than in external observances. According to the parable of the Pharisee and the publican, the kingdom of God is more

Our ideas of God and the kingdom need to be expanded and to grow continuously.

available in everyday life, with its routines, failures, disappointments, joys, and successes than in sacred places, shrines, and rituals. It becomes present to us and in us by our consent and by the dispositions that the Holy Spirit instills within us, the chief of which is faith that God is truly and secretly intervening to heal us despite any and all appearances to the contrary.

✠

Was God present to Jesus when he abandoned him on the cross? Is he with us as we struggle with tragedy or with impossible situations? Apocalyptic myths look for a savior to resolve all problems. But to resolve all problems is to miss the point. The kingdom is manifested by our attitude toward our problems, not by their disappearance. That is how Jesus sanctifies the outcasts and whatever is outcast in us.

What idea of the kingdom begins to emerge as we listen attentively to the parable of the leaven? It is that the leaven, moral corruption, is not always replaced by the unleavened bread, the symbol of the holy; that daily problems are not normally changed by any divine intervention that we can see or feel. Hope is the grace that trusts God in the midst of everydayness with its ever-recurring trips to nowhere and the recycling of the same old temptations. We are left with the hope of transformation, but without any experience of it happening.

Eight

THE BARREN FIG TREE

"A MAN HAD A FIG TREE PLANTED *in his vineyard; and he came looking for fruit on it and found none. So he said to the gardener, 'See here! For three years I have come looking for fruit on this fig tree, and still I find none. Cut it down! Why should it be wasting the soil?' He replied, 'Sir, let it alone for one more year, until I dig around it and put some manure on it. If it bears fruit next year, well and good; but if not, you can cut it down.'"*
(Luke 13:6–9)

The parable of the barren fig tree recalls the recurrent theme in the Old Testament of the barren made fruitful by the Lord's direct intervention. The birth of John the Baptist is the classic example. His mother by the power of God became fertile in her old age, and to the astonishment of everyone, brought forth the child who would become the greatest of the prophets. Rachel, the beloved of Isaac, like Sarah, the wife of

Abraham, was also barren until she was made fruitful by God.

The expectation of the original hearers of this parable, then, would be that God will intervene and turn this wretched tree, that has not produced any fruit for three years, into a flourishing tree bearing a superabundance of figs. In the Old Testament, the fig tree was the symbol of God's blessing and special love for God's people.

✥ *The divine presence is so present that nothing can take it from us.*

The gardener suggests putting some manure around the ailing plant. A delicate touch! The text uses a more refined word, "manure," but the actual meaning is closer to "dung." Hardly a decorous word in religious discourse, but Jesus did not hesitate to use it. It adds a certain earthiness—if not outright pungency—to the story.

What are we left with at the conclusion of this parable? A tree that is good for nothing. The gardener offers to shovel manure around it, but there is no indication that any new growth will actually occur. This tree and its predicament are striking symbols of daily life, especially when our efforts to do good fail or seem to be fruitless, our prayer periods are as dry as dust, and nothing ever happens. In addition, there is

no sense of God's presence in daily life, no enlightenment experience, while our faults continue, people
blame us unjustly, and disappointments multiply. Our
spiritual life seems to be dead. What are we to do?
The parable seems to say, just keep waiting.

This parable hints that it does not matter if we do not
succeed in our own estimation or in that of others.
The divine presence is so present that nothing can
take it from us. Of course, we can still reject God, but
someone who is seeking God is not about to do that.
When we realize the fact of God's closeness, success
and failure are relativized. We simply do what we can:
that is, we throw a little manure—symbol of our fruitless efforts—on the old stick. Of course it is not going
to grow, because it is dead. But in some mysterious
way, because of God's solidarity with us in everyday
life, something much more important happens.

This parable addresses something very deep in human
nature and in the best of people. It is the perplexing
question, "Why, when I do my best to pray, to do
good, and to try to get closer to God, make sacrifices
for others and put up with all kinds of trials, am I so
beset with troubles, break an arm or a leg, turn up
with some debilitating disease, lose a loved one, go
through a painful divorce, live at the edge of finan-
cial ruin, or fall into some grievous addiction?" In
other words, "Are life's reverses signs of God's pun-

ishment for my moral lapses, or are they just tests of my patience? Can I hope that God will eventually reward me with some high state of perfection or rescue me from my troubles by means of some apocalyptic deliverance?"

The parable suggests that Jesus does not recommend that we count on either expectation. Meanwhile, we reach out desperately for something to lean on in the face of difficulties, reverses, and heartbreaks.

✤

In the light of the parables, it is a mistake to aim at a mystical state that we can feel, understand, and enjoy, all of which easily give rise to the temptation to feel superior to others. Jesus nowhere represents mystical union as the goal of the kingdom—still less, the prayer of quiet or the prayer of union. And less still, various supernatural interventions such as locutions, ecstasies, visions, charismatic gifts, and spiritual highs. These all feed into the naive idea that the kingdom of God will solve all problems, put "me" in a place beyond the everyday, the normal, and the nitty-gritty—in short, that the purpose of the kingdom of God is to make "me"

✤ *The God of pure faith is closer than breathing, closer than thinking, closer than choosing, closer than consciousness itself.*

feel special. We *are* special, but not because of those things. What is special about us is God's incredible solidarity with our ordinary lives: with our sense of failure, futility, getting nowhere spiritually, and our lack of inner resources to cope with our particular difficulties. In the parables daily life is so clearly the place where the kingdom is working that symbols of success are totally irrelevant. They are like icing on a cake. We cannot live on icing. We need more substantial food. Trust in God disregards the evidence of everyday life that God is absent or forgetful of us and brings us into direct contact with the God of everyday. The God of pure faith is so close: closer than breathing, closer than thinking, closer than choosing, closer than consciousness itself.

An enlightened faith seems very ordinary. One might scarcely notice it. It accepts the way things are and finds God vibrantly present in the most insignificant situations and in the most unexpected disguises. "Dung" in this parable is the symbol of humble hope, which keeps trusting in God without trying to analyze or resolve the tension between the hard realities of everyday life and God's sovereignty.

In a world in which God seems to be absent, people have to conjure up ideal situations in order to help themselves survive. And so poets and seers elaborate myths, one of which for religious people at least is to pass into a world of moral perfection, wisdom, and bliss; the other is to await the apocalyptic vindication of one's nation, race, ethnic group, religion, or bedraggled reputation.

✥

Does the death and resurrection of Jesus offer a new myth into which we can escape by moving into an idealized state of perfection or into some apocalyptic deliverance? Not according to the parables. And not according to the crucifixion narratives of the synoptic Gospels in which Jesus' abandonment by the Father—"My God, my God, why have you forsaken me?"—seems to question his very identity as the Son of God.

✥ *The essence of contemplative prayer is not spiritual experience, but the purification of the unconscious.*

The divine emptiness of Jesus is the point at which the power and mercy of the kingdom are maximized. We experience the same divine emptiness in our daily lives as we wait for something to happen that will fix everything that seems wrong in our particular environment or in us. Jesus in the parables affirms, "The kingdom is right where you are with your bundle of difficulties, your sense of getting nowhere and waiting in prayer for experiences that never happen." Divine union is not the achievement of some perfection of our own or an escape from our external problems, but is the radical change of attitude that enables us to deal effectively with our weaknesses and our problems—the humble acceptance of our lives just as they are, including the monumental moral corruption we may find in ourselves.

This experience of failure can cause no little disappointment and disillusionment. But disappointment in *what* is the question we have to ask. The answer is usually to be found in our deep-seated expectations, of course. Divine love is not normally going to change the situation by some great miracle. It is trying to change us, so that we can courageously and lovingly unite ourselves to God in the situation.

It is a mistake, then, to look for spiritual experiences in contemplative prayer or to judge our progress by them. The essence of contemplative prayer is not spiritual experience, but the purification of the unconscious. That process, usually quite lengthy, is what radically changes our attitudes and enables us to see ourselves as we truly are. Contemplation must not be presented as a road to glory. It is easy to become attached to spiritual experiences. The regular practice of contemplative prayer initiates the purification of the unconscious with all its repressed emotional pain: anger, shame, grief, fear, discouragement. Our experience, therefore, is not likely to be of an abundant harvest of delicious figs, but rather of "the dung."

Gardening is the first job that Adam was given in the garden of Eden; it is the symbol of what everybody's job is: shoveling manure to make the unfruitful fig tree (us) bloom. It will never bloom because of the manure, but God, touched by our persevering efforts and patient endurance, may make the thing blossom anyway—not because of our efforts and patience, but because of God's most tender love for us.

What happens to the barren fig tree if there is no one, like this concerned gardener, to take an interest in it and to try to save it?

Part Two

GOD LOVES
INFINITELY
AND ALWAYS

THE PRODIGAL SON 1

"A MAN HAD TWO SONS, *and the younger son said to his father, 'Father, give me the share of your estate that should come to me.' So the father divided the property between them. After a few days, the younger son collected all his belongings and set off to a distant country where he squandered his inheritance in a life of dissipation. When he had freely spent everything, a severe famine struck that country, and he found himself in dire need. So he hired himself out to one of the local citizens who sent him to his farm to tend the swine. And he longed to eat his fill of the pods on which the swine fed, but nobody gave him any. Coming to his senses he thought, 'How many of my father's hired workers have more than enough food to eat, but here am I, dying from hunger. I shall get up and go to my father and I shall say to him, "Father, I have sinned against heaven and against you. I no longer deserve to be called your son; treat me as you would treat one of your hired workers."' So he got up and went back to his father. While he was still a long way off, his father caught sight of him, and was filled with compassion. He ran to his son, embraced him and kissed him. His son said to him, 'Father, I have sinned against heaven and against you; I no longer deserve to be called your son.' But his father ordered his servants, 'Quickly bring the finest robe and put it on him; put a ring on his fingers and sandals on his feet. Take the fattened calf and slaughter it. Then let us celebrate with a feast, because this son of mine was dead, and has come to life again; he was lost, and has been found.' Then the celebration began." (Luke 15:11–24)*

Here we see a young man who obviously has an enormous emotional investment in having a good time. He had been saving up his money and now has the inheritance he asked for. His drive for happiness centers around pleasure, affection, and esteem. So he gathers his possessions and heads off for the good life. While he is out on his prolonged toot, his emotional program for pleasure does not work out as well as expected. In the midst of his enjoyment of the high life comes a great famine; he loses all his money, his friends desert him, and he has nothing to eat. Out of desperation he takes the job of herdsman in a pigsty. In the local culture this was the lowest form of earning a living. At this point, he remembers how well fed everybody was at home including the hired servants. Notice that his motive for going home was not the best. His chief reason is that his program for happiness based on pleasure was not viable.

This parable communicates the fact that we are relating with a God who is infinitely concerned. The father of the prodigal was waiting for years for his son

✢ True security, independence, and affection were all present in his father's house.

to wake up and realize that happiness is not to be found in the pursuit of pleasure. When he sees his son heading home, he is deeply moved. In fact, he is so touched by the sight of this bedraggled child on his way home that he forgets about the shabby way the boy had treated him when he went off with his share of the inheritance. He rushes out to meet him and heaps all kinds of welcome on him.

This parable is addressed to people who are living a life that the general public regards as disreputable. Most sinners, at a deep level, are insecure, lonely, and usually acting out the damage done to them in early life. Their actual conduct is not so much their choice as the result of desperate attempts to deal with the overwhelming emotional trauma inflicted on them by adults at an age when they could not handle it. This father's one concern is to reinstate his son. The son's hope is to get a position among the hired hands where he would get enough to eat. That is the extent of his trust in his father. The reception he received must have come as a shock to him. He suddenly realizes that he has never understood his father or the extent of his father's love for him, never fathomed his father's concern and depth of forgiveness.

✠

This parable is aimed at the hearts of people who have lost hope and whose despair is expressed in the constant repetition of lifestyles that cannot bring happiness. Yet they are locked into them because they do not know the happiness found in God's friendship that would pull them out of the vicious circle of desire, gratification, and frustration—the endless cycle of craving and disappointment. The father was ready to forgive and forget everything in his delight in finding the son who was lost. Going into a far country in search of happiness was a tragedy because true security, independence, and affection were all present in his father's house and the prodigal son did not know it.

The sinners who are listening to Jesus are being invited into the same boundless forgiveness. It is not merit that brings one into the friendship of this father but consent to his infinite goodness and concern.
What do we do after we have come home, after we have chosen once again to live under the gaze of God's infinite tenderness instead of hiding from it? What do we do with feelings of greed, pride, vainglory, jealousy, envy, lust, wanting to manipulate

other people, or in short, with the whole world of selfishness that does not belong in the father's house?

This return to the father's house is not the return to heaven. It is only a return to the right orientation of our lives with all the damage that we bring with us from early childhood. Once we have chosen the orientation of living in the father's house, the symbol of God's presence, Jesus joins us wherever we are. The acts of selfishness, backward glances, regressive tendencies to former emotional states are all something that we share with Christ and he with us. He identifies with our personal history in every detail. Instead of thinking we are alienated from God when afflictive emotions arise, we realize that they are fuel for divine love. We can then welcome them without identifying with them because we see them as wounds that God is trying to heal.

In this story nothing is said about the boy's mother. The father seems to be a single parent, both mother and father to his sons. Perhaps the mother's absence was the boy's basic problem from the moment he started out in life. Our mother is our first window onto God, and if this window is missing because of misunderstandings, physical absence, or inadequate parenting, the window is hard to open later in life. The vocation of a mother must be one of the greatest vocations there is. Starting out well in life would solve an enormous number of problems.

Ten

THE REIGN OF GOD 1

(The Hidden Treasure, The Pearl, and The Net)

"THE KINGDOM OF HEAVEN *is like a treasure buried in a field, which a person finds and hides again, and out of joy goes and sells all that he has and buys that field. Again, the kingdom of heaven is like a merchant searching for fine pearls. When he finds a pearl of great price, he goes and sells all that he has and buys it. Again, the kingdom of heaven is like a net thrown into the sea, which collects fish of every kind. When it is full they haul it ashore and sit down to put what is good into buckets. What is bad they throw away. Thus it will be at the end of the age. The angels will go out and separate the wicked from the righteous and throw them into the fiery furnace, where there will be wailing and grinding of teeth.*

"Do you understand all these things?" They answered, "Yes." And he replied, "Then every scribe who has been instructed in the kingdom of heaven is like the head of a household who brings from his storeroom both the new

and the old." When Jesus finished these parables, he went away from there. (Matthew 13:44–54)

The parables in this series in Matthew 13, each in its own way, reflect a certain light on the reign of God. The first parable is about one who discovered buried treasure in a field. At the time of the Gospel, this was not unusual. In days gone by, people used to bury their treasures to protect them. This man was lucky enough to hit a treasure chest while plowing a field. He went and bought the field.

Another man was looking for fine pearls, and when he found one, he sold everything and bought that pearl. The reign of God is the pearl of great price or the treasure hidden in the field. The reign of God is the discovery of the divine presence and action within us. The reign of God is happiness. If you find the reign of God, you don't need anything else; it relativizes all other treasures. It is the focusing of one's value system. Jesus describes this focusing in another parable as a single eye. It is the purity of intention that arises not by our efforts but by the discovery of the divine presence within. This is the gift, but it does not take effect until we awaken to its presence and submit to its action.

The key to happiness is the presence of God as a growing conviction, as a presence that integrates and penetrates all our activity, transforming every human

❖ *If you find the reign of God, you don't need anything else; it relativizes all other treasures.*

faculty and potentiality. The true Self is the divine presence within us working through our particular uniqueness. Intentionality, then, is basically the orientation to the treasure within us, to the pearl of great price, which is the awareness of the divine presence and action within.

This is the focus of the centering prayer practice. We do not constantly recreate our intention. In these parables, these people didn't keep digging for treasure or keep buying the same pearl again and again. They committed themselves once and for all because of the value they saw in their discoveries. Once we have chosen the reign of God and decided to pursue it, it becomes the basic source out of which all our actions emerge, the good soil in which the divine seed grows.

Intentionality connects to the divine energy within us. In centering prayer we immerse ourselves in our commitment to Christ, in our original intention of buying the pearl and of plugging into the reign of God. It is not so much we who initiate; rather, we consent to God's presence and action within us. We consent to God's intentionality. As Paul says, "In love he destined us for adoption to himself through Jesus Christ, in accord with the favor of his will" (Eph. 1:5). So the intention that enables us to enter the reign of God is not a bright idea of our own. It is rather submission to the divine intentionality that is calling us into the kingdom.

The more focused our intention, the more powerful it is. Our intention is submission to God's intention. We are not the generators of our good works or of our relationship with God. We perceive, rather, that we are receivers of the divine life, which does not belong to us, but which is entrusted to us if we consent.

✠

We come now to the parable of the net thrown into the sea that pulled in all kinds of fish. Notice that it was not pulled in until it was filled. This is a revelation of how the reign of God works; it does not come to us prepackaged with our name on it. It evolves. The human condition is like the net full of fish and various kinds of junk that have been thrown into the sea. The junk is precisely what the Spirit separates out in the dark nights. The Spirit puts the good stuff into containers and throws out the rest. The Spirit works through our personal history layer by layer, preserving the values of each stage and throwing out what is worthless. This separation does not occur until the Spirit has moved us to the decisive moment of harvesting, which takes place when the Spirit's work of purifying our unconscious has reached a certain completion. Then we can say with St. John of the Cross, "My one activity is love." What other ministry is there? Whatever else we do, unless it comes from that intentionality, is more or less ineffective.

The Cloud of Unknowing makes a distinction between acts of will and love. Love is the abiding intentionality out of which particular acts of will emerge. In this situation, whatever one does has the effectiveness of apostolic love, a term that the early monastic fathers used to refer to the love the apostles experienced when the Holy Spirit took possession of them at Pentecost. That is the source of every true apostolate.

Eleven

THE REIGN OF GOD 2

(The Hidden Treasure, The Pearl, and The Net)

"THE KINGDOM OF HEAVEN IS LIKE *a treasure buried in a field, which a person finds and hides again, and out of joy goes and sells all that he has and buys that field. Again, the kingdom of heaven is like a merchant searching for fine pearls. When he finds a pearl of great price, he goes and sells all that he has and buys it. Again, the kingdom of heaven is like a net thrown into the sea, which collects fish of every kind. When it is full they haul it ashore and sit down to put what is good into buckets. What is bad they throw away. Thus it will be at the end of the age. The angels will go out and separate the wicked from the righteous and throw them into the fiery furnace, where there will be wailing and grinding of teeth.*

"Do you understand all these things?" They answered, "Yes." And he replied, "Then every scribe who has been instructed in the kingdom of heaven is like the head of a household who brings from his storeroom both the new

and the old." When Jesus finished these parables, he went away from there. (Matthew 13:44–54)

As Jesus concluded these arresting parables in Matthew 13, he asked the crowd with a great sense of ✤ *The living tradition alone passes on the full Christian life.* irony, "Do you understand?" They said, "Yes!" He then said: "Every scribe learned in the reign of God knows how to bring forth out of his treasures new things and old." Some people can bring out all kinds of new things, but very little out of tradition. And some people can bring out the old stuff ad nauseam. Neither are teachers that Jesus considers apt for the reign of God. Fidelity to the old and openness to the new were magnificently represented by Pope John XXIII. The signs of the times that he recommended to the consideration of the bishops at the Vatican Council are a revelation of God just as much as things long since past. The living tradition alone passes on the full Christian life. The church constantly has to integrate new wisdom, new science, new information into the Gospel if she is going to communicate it to contemporary people and to people of other cultures. Unfortunately, those of little faith tend to identify the values of the Gospel with particular structures or symbols. Then if the symbol is modified, like turning the altar around or receiving communion in the hand, they think the values of the Gospel are being rejected.

People have to grow beyond this over-identification. Ancient symbols can sometimes prevent the value of the Gospel from being fully transmitted in new circumstances. Even words develop opposite meanings over time. Would we say that Jesus was not in continuity with Moses and the prophets? They bore witness to him on the mountain. Yet he was completely free about following their tradition. He paid no attention to the rabbinical practices of preaching only in synagogues and only with regard to scripture.

⁂

It is precisely the intentionality of love that goes beyond human rules, customs, and mindsets and enables the church to present the message of the Gospel in the way that it can best be heard in particular circumstances of time and place. When this hasn't been done, as we read again and again in history, the moment of grace is lost to the church. In China, the Jesuit Father Matteo Ricci intuited the way to present the Gospel to the Buddhists. He was accepted by the people. His influence was growing. But one of the other orders couldn't bear to see a Jesuit missionary succeeding. History gives us the mournful news that they succeeded in obtaining from the Roman authorities the suppression of the mission. So Ricci came home and so did the Gospel. If he had been allowed to continue, who knows what the later history of China might have been? He was ahead of his time. Maybe we should say that certain people in the church were behind the times. Or as Pope John XXIII would have said, they could not read the signs of the times. Jesus expects us to discern how the Gospel is to be transmitted once we have absorbed and assimilated it through *lectio divina,* prayer, and the service of community.

The reign of God involves a social dimension, not just the sifting of our own motivation. It involves the ability to sift the wheat from the chaff. Many religious communities today are trying to recover their charism and to discern what they were sent by the Spirit to do, and not just keep doing what they happen to be doing because of historical conditions. Jesus recommends this discernment for the building up of his body the church, to which we have a responsibility to share whatever we have been given.

Twelve

THE SOWER

"A SOWER WENT OUT TO SOW. *And as he sowed, some seed fell on the path and birds came and ate it up. Some fell on rocky ground, where it had little soil. It sprang up at once because the soil was not deep, and when the sun rose it was scorched, and it withered for lack of roots. Some seed fell among thorns, and the thorns grew up and choked it. But some seed fell on rich soil, and produced fruit, a hundred or sixty or thirtyfold. Whoever has ears ought to hear." (Matthew 13:1–9)*

In the parable of the sower Jesus seems to be referring to his own preaching. Some of the seed, he says, falls on the path, that is, on the hardpan, the path that goes through the field but that has no give, no flexibility, and is almost as hard as concrete. To translate that into modern terms, the word of God sometimes falls on the sidewalks of New York or Amarillo, to mention only two great cities. There is no chance of this seed bearing fruit because it can't get through the concrete. The concrete represents the mythic membership level of consciousness and the worldviews in which people live with unquestioning presuppositions and preconceived ideas: the world of racism, sexism, prejudice, and every kind of bias.

We have to take for granted that we bring to our listening to the word of God a certain amount of hardpan in our consciousness, made up of the unquestioned values and assumptions of parents, peer groups, and teachers that we absorbed in early childhood, especially during the socialization period from four to ten. All of these powerful influences have programmed our understanding of reality.

The parables are earthquakes shaking the ground from under our presuppositions and prepackaged values in order that a few cracks in the sidewalk might appear, enabling some of the seed to fall in between the cracks and produce at least a few weeds. The upsetting of our preconceived ideas is not a disaster; it is a necessity in order to hear the word of God. Thus, trials that upset our preconceived values are a great gift from God. Notice the succinctness of this one sentence: "Some seed fell on the path." It addresses one obstacle to the hearing of the word of God as it is sown and not according to our interpretation. The interpretation is often not our own, but one we have absorbed from other people, our culture, ethnic group, and early religious training.

Let's look at the fate of the other seed. "Some fell on rocky ground." New England farms bring forth a new crop of rocks every spring no matter how many one picks up the previous year. That's why you have rock walls everywhere in New England. Although the word of God may be received with a certain openness, there is no substance to rocky soil. The seed when it grows up can't withstand the wind, the heat, and the rain. Perhaps this image points to those rocks in us that are compulsive activity or habits that resist change.

Some seeds fell on fertile soil, but there were already other things there, namely thorns, thistles, and weeds. When the word of God started to grow, it was choked by the lure of money, power, and plea-sure-seeking.

Finally, some seed fell on good soil: not much in the way of weeds or briars, with depth to it and a looseness into which the seed could sink its roots. The soil suggests receptivity. The other soils were receptive too, but because of their varying forms of resistance, the word could not get through.

�֍

The parables are not moralistic. They are earth-shattering. They break up our prepackaged values and preconceived ideas and thus raise the fundamental question addressed to Adam and Eve after the Fall: "Where are you?"

The answer is we are in one of those four categories. We are confronted by reality in the parables in a way that forces us to enter into ourselves and to ask the right questions. We want to do good and we don't. We don't want to do bad and we do. That's the situation. The only answer is to turn over our unmanageable lives to the Higher Power.

When we come to contemplative prayer we are talking about the divine seed in its most pure form. The word of God is addressing now with a certain vigor �֍ *"Where are you?"* each of those areas in us that resemble the different kinds of soil that Jesus differentiates in the parable. The divine light attacks whatever is resistant in us. There is something in us that does not quite want to let go. We want to hear, but just so much. We want to loosen up our hardpan, but not yet! Yes, we are open, except for... We want to give in, but do we? And so the great question, "Where are you?" arises with great urgency. Hanging on? Resisting? Loving the old pre-suppositions that seem to provide some security? Or still locked into the emotional programs for happiness?

Since we won't let go in some areas, the Divine Therapist keeps bringing up the same old issues. Relentlessly. Tenderly but firmly; consoling but also tough at times. The pain of realizing that something has to go that we love, are attached to, and depend on keeps gnawing away.

How much do we want to hear the word of God? That is the question. "Will this ultimate confrontation wipe me out? Will my self, that dear thing that I love so much—that causes me nothing but pain, but still the only self I know—have to go? Where will I be? Where will I go?"

"*Where* are you?"

THE WIDOW AND THE UNJUST JUDGE

"THERE WAS A JUDGE *in a certain town who neither feared God nor respected any human being. And a widow in that town used to come to him and say, 'Render a just decision for me against my adversary.' For a long time the judge was unwilling, but eventually he thought, 'While it is true that I neither fear God nor respect any human being, because this widow keeps bothering me I shall deliver a just decision for her lest she finally come and strike me.'" The Lord said, "Pay attention to what the dishonest judge says. Will not God then secure the rights of his chosen ones who call out to him day and night? Will he be slow to answer them? I tell you, he will see to it that justice is done for them speedily. But when the Son of Man comes, will he find faith on earth?"* (Luke 18:1–8)

The purpose of this parable is to encourage us to pray continuously and not to lose heart, to keep asking for what we need. It is a far-out tale with a certain humor about it that is characteristic of the parables. The widow is a symbol of everyone in some kind of need. She evidently was being pursued by her insurance company. She was pounding on the door of this judge saying, "Help, help, help! I need this money and this company is after it. Do me justice."

The judge couldn't care less about justice, God, or this lady's plight. He was only interested in himself. She finally wore him out by pounding on his door, calling him on the phone, sending him telegrams. Finally he said, "I can't put up with this anymore. I'll let her win the case because I'm fed up with being pursued day and night by her persistence." That is a humorous way of presenting the goodness of God. We don't often think of God that way. If we just badger God enough, God will respond. So gimme, gimme, gimme has a certain power according to this text. Jesus says, "Don't give up. If this unjust judge finally caved in, will not God in his goodness provide the help that you need if you keep asking?"

Why doesn't God answer us more promptly? Why do we have to wait so long and why don't we get more of the things that we ask for?

✣

There is another place in scripture in which Jesus seems to take the role of a severe judge. That is the situation in which the Canaanite woman came asking for the cure of her daughter.

Since Jesus had provided all kinds of miraculous cures, she didn't expect to meet with any hesitation. He didn't respond to her at *✣ "Will not God in his goodness provide the help that you need if you keep asking?"* all, even when the apostles interceded on her behalf. He didn't reply when she prostrated herself with her nose in the dust and pleaded. When she persisted, he insulted her saying that it was not possible to give the food of the children to dogs. She received from him silence, insult, and rejection; yet she kept waiting, hoping, and asking. At last she said, "I'm not asking for much, just a few crumbs. Forget about the bread." This is the faith that finally cracked the armor of God. Jesus exclaimed, "Your faith is great indeed! You can have anything you want!"

Notice it was only after silence, insult, rejection, and the apparent failure of her prayer that Jesus acted. This delay is not an infrequent experience of sincere seekers of God when they have what seems to them to be a very important need. The Canaanite woman just kept hanging on. Notice that her physical position moved from standing to kneeling to prostrating, a symbol perhaps that this silence of God was doing an enormous amount of constructive work by increasing her faith and bringing it to the one-pointedness that pierced through every obstacle and touched the heart of God.

Silence is one answer to prayer. God responds not so much by granting individual requests but by changing us from inside. Prayer is not designed to change God or the situation, but to change us. If the external circumstances are helpful to that end, we may receive our request. If there is a possibility that our faith will grow in this mysterious dialogue between our petitions and the divine silence, we may not have our request granted. In other words, prayer is designed to increase faith, which is not a particular petition for anything, but the total surrender of ourselves to God. Faith means entrusting the whole of ourselves to the infinite mercy of God. It is a continual prayer. The particular favors that concern us often belong to an immature level of faith. The dialogue between the Canaanite woman and Jesus is also our experience of prayer over a number of years, perhaps twenty or thirty, in which as a result of persevering, God brings us to the fundamental attitude of prayer that is not a particular petition, but an attitude of total receptivity to the primary message of the universe, which is love. That message produces the kingdom both in us and outside. The reign of God isn't just in us; it is also everywhere else. By accessing it in ourselves, we can perceive it everywhere else.

✥

Faith dissolves the enormous illusion of the human condition, which is that God is absent. This great lie, the source of all human misery, prevents the free flow of the divine life and love into us and into the world. The purpose of continuous prayer is to access that which is most true about us, namely, our divine Source. The divine is always manifesting itself, though mostly in secret, to those who walk in the presence of God and allow this presence to influence all their relationships.

Fourteen

THE WORKMEN
IN THE VINEYARD

"FOR THE KINGDOM OF HEAVEN *is like a land-owner who went out early in the morning to hire laborers for his vineyard. After agreeing with the laborers for the usual daily wage, he sent them into his vineyard. When he went out about nine o'clock, he saw others standing idle in the marketplace; and to them he said, 'You also go into the vineyard, and I will pay you whatever is right.' So they went. When he went out again about noon and about three o'clock, he did the same. And about five o'clock he went and found others standing around; and he said to them, 'Why are you standing here idle all day?' They said to him, 'Because no one has hired us.' He said to them, 'You also go into the vineyard.' When evening came, the owner of the vineyard said to his manager, 'Call the laborers and give them their pay, beginning with the last then going to the first.' When those hired about five o'clock came, each of them received the usual daily wage. Now when the first came, they thought they would receive more; but each of them also received the usual daily wage. And when they received it, they grumbled against the landowner, saying, 'These last worked only one hour, and you have made them equal to us who have born the burden of the day and the scorching heat.' But he replied to one of them, 'Friend, I am doing you no wrong; did you not agree with me for the usual daily wage? Take what belongs to you and go; I choose to give to this last as I give to you. Am I not allowed to do what I choose with what belongs to me? Or are you envious because I am generous?'" (Matthew 20:1–15)*

The householder was not generous in regard to the wages he offered to the first workers, which was only a denarius, the subsistence wage for peasants. They worked a twelve-hour day in the scorching heat.

At intervals during the day the householder went to the marketplace and hired more people. This time he did not negotiate. He simply said, "I will pay you what is right." There was no contract, just the hope that he would give them some reasonable remuneration. At the eleventh hour he went out again and found a few idlers who had been hanging around all day. By this time a good number of them were probably well into their cups. So they stumbled into the vineyard, picked a grape or two, and then it was time to quit.

The householder says to the steward, "Pay the last ones a denarius." This seems like a sign of great generosity on the part of the householder. But his generosity runs out when the ones who worked all day come forward only to get the same amount. They grumble because they expected to receive more.

The householder's behavior seems unjust. The hearers would naturally side with the workers who felt they were mistreated, even though they received what they contracted for. This parable raises questions about the standard of justice in the kingdom of God. Should not those who worked more hours have been given more? Evidently, entry into the kingdom of God is not a question of merit.

Human standards of judgment are subverted in this parable. Ordinary standards of justice cannot explain how the kingdom works. Paul discusses this problem at length in the third chapter of Romans where he points out that God does not distinguish between persons. Justification and sanctification are gifts and have nothing to do with social status or personal merit. The teaching of this parable is extremely important for those on the spiritual journey. Over centuries a secular standard of values crept into Christian teaching in the form of an elaborate system of earning heavenly rewards. Hence if we were trained in pre-Vatican II Catholicism, for example, we might feel challenged or even dismayed by this parable. We were taught that by going to Mass on Sunday, spending time in prayer and spiritual reading, frequenting the sacraments, giving alms during Lent, abstaining from meat on Fridays, and so forth, we would pile up merits so that the punishment due to our sins would be canceled out. That teaching has been downplayed since the Second Vatican Council, but the temptation remains for people of various faiths on the spiritual journey, particularly if their experience of prayer is going well. If we enjoy special favors, we might be in great trouble. We might slip into the presumption that our good deeds had earned those gifts. Hence the necessity of trusting in God's mercy and not in our own spiritual experiences or accomplishments.

✛

How do we get into the kingdom if it is not something that we can earn? We enter the kingdom not by meriting but by consenting to the invitation. In the parable, grace is symbolized by the mysterious need of the householder for more workers, and it seems to be urgent, manifested by the fact that he went out every couple of hours to find more workers. Those who accepted his invitation entered, and at the end of the day all received the same recompense. Grace is God's need to respond to our need. The inner nature of God is thus made manifest to us: God has to respond, so to speak, to our needs. In this parable God's response is directed to the people standing there in the marketplace, idle and wasting their time, gambling, drinking, gossiping, snoozing, or whatever.

Jesus in this parable seems to be trying to justify his practice of reaching out to outcasts and sinners. Their behavior does not merit anything, but their need is great. It is their need that he, as God's son, is responding to. Hence his behavior subverts our idea of how to win God's favor. We do not. God's favor and mercy is evoked in direct proportion to our destitution—to our lack of inner and outer resources. Our need is what creates God's need to reach out to us, even if we do not realize how needy we actually are.

The invitation of grace to enter the kingdom goes forth again and again and again. No one is forced to accept. The invitation is extended because of the total largesse and goodness of God. The very definition of mercy is that it responds to need. Infinite mercy of its very nature has to reach out to need. God's greatest gift (response to our need) is, of course, to offer us the divine life itself. This is why Jesus reached out to public sinners. In manifesting the heart of the Father, he had to show the Father's urgent concern for those most in need of his grace and help. Grace and help, of course, are just as gratuitous for the well-behaved.

Respectable folks in general do not like this parable. By respectable I mean those who observe the norms of conventional society, but who are unaware of how much their unconscious programs for happiness are at work in their lives, and how significant a part of

✥ *The invitation of grace to enter the kingdom goes forth again and again and again.*

their good deeds are secretly motivated by the desire for acclaim, power, or security. The false self easily adjusts to whatever our cultural mindset may be and co-opts good deeds as easily as the not-so-good. On the spiritual journey we need to be alert to our secret motivation. Although self-knowledge does not cure the disease, at least it disposes us to work toward heal-ing, because it shows us the harm we are doing to ourselves and to others. In trying to face the dark side of our personalities, mixed motivation, and the dam-age done to us in early childhood, our attitude toward our very real limitations is more important than their healing. Indeed, it is a major part of our healing.

The bottom line of this teaching is that the kingdom is not based on human standards of justice and equity, but on the infinite mercy of God whose principal need is to respond to the desperate state of the human condition.

The fallen human condition is where the kingdom is most active. We are the people for whom Jesus Christ has come in the flesh to express the infinite concern of the Father for our sins and their consequences. The

✣ *Spiritual progress is the sheer gift of God.* spiritual journey enables us to appreciate more and more the total gratuity of the divine goodness. Acceptance of the invitation is the key to belonging to the kingdom. We are not prize packages. We recognize that boundless compassion is the way God is. It is because God is our Father and Mother that we are invited into the kingdom. That is why our self-generated projects for holiness are questionable and why we need to cultivate a disposition of receptivity and openness to the Holy Spirit. Reason will not get us there. Good deeds will not get us there. The kingdom is sheer gift.

✣

The problem of a faithful and virtuous life, as Scott points out, is that it creates the sense of having earned something from God and thus misses the invitation. Justification does not come through good works but through the divine largesse. Good deeds are essential, but only insofar as they manifest our good will. Spiritual progress is the sheer gift of God. God is not waiting to crown us with a halo for our good deeds. God is waiting to forgive us for our sins and press us to heart as little children in desperate need of boundless love. This parable announces that human standards of judgment have no place in the kingdom. A new standard is present, which is God's infinite need to show mercy.

THE HIDDEN TREASURE

"THE KINGDOM OF HEAVEN *is like a treasure hidden in a field, which someone found and hid; then in his joy he goes and sells all that he has and buys that field."*
(Matthew 13:44)

The word parable means "laid beside." So the kingdom of God is known by laying it beside certain symbols or signs. Unlike a simile, the parable actually *contains* the truth revealed by the comparison. Hence the parables are not just comparisons or something like something else. The kingdom really *is* the way that Jesus presents it.

Here the kingdom of God is presented as a treasure. That in itself is not unusual. In the book of Wisdom, wisdom is looked upon as a treasure that has to be sought. But what is unusual—and problematic—is what happens in this parable once the treasure is found.

The man in this brief tale was probably a day laborer. In those days, people did not always have a bank handy. Because of the vicissitudes of the times, they sometimes hid their treasures in a field, hoping to return later in a period of peace to dig them up. Thus it was not unusual for a day laborer working in somebody else's field to come upon a buried treasure. This man hid the treasure again, and then went off and bought the field. The hearers are left with the problem of evaluating the morality of his conduct. If he owned the field, there would be no sense in hiding the treasure. If he had a just claim to the treasure, why would he hide it again? There is clearly an element of scandal in his behavior.

How can the kingdom of God be compared to a treasure that gives rise to such improper conduct? In rabbinical law, if it was not clear who owned the treasure, the owner of the field was presumed to own it. Evidently this man hid it because he was trying to conceal it from its rightful owner.

In the more elaborate version of this parable in the Gospel of Thomas, after the man buried the treasure, he becomes a money lender. So we may think, "Finding a buried treasure for this man must be like winning the state lottery today." Although the lottery is not a buried treasure and one never really expects to win, somebody, in fact, always wins. In any case, this parable is about a similar situation. The treasure is there before the man finds it. This is an important aspect of the kingdom of God. It is in the world and available through the preaching of the gospel. Thus we might find it without intending to—by accident, so to speak.

This man had no test of his virtue but simply found the treasure. His capacity to make good use of his find was thus based on a shaky moral foundation. God has taken a similar risk with each of us. The Father has made the treasure of grace available through the incarnation of his Son, Jesus Christ, but we do not know how to use it. In fact, we are not even remotely prepared for the responsibilities that this treasure involves. Hence we may use the treasure improperly, or the treasure itself may become a scandal for us.

The man in the parable in his joy went and sold all he had and bought the field. Once it is safely concealed in the field, he cannot dig it up again without people wondering how he got it. Though he has the treasure, he is more impoverished than before, because he has now sold all his other possessions. He winds up with an enormous treasure that he cannot do anything with.

The parable alerts us to the fact that the kingdom, although it is given us as sheer gift, is not given to us just for our personal benefit. To share this gift with others is an essential part of receiving it. Not doing so will engage us in some form of scandal, especially if we try to use it only for ourselves.

Since the kingdom comes to us as a great treasure without our having earned it, we do not value it in the same way that we would if we had been forced to seek it. The scandal, then, is that God freely gives us such an abundance of grace that we do not place enough value on it and fail to grasp our responsibilities to make use of it for the community. The treasure, when not used for others, becomes a source of scandal for us. If we use it for purely selfish motives, all the ways in which the false self manifests itself in worldly ways under a religious or spiritual disguise are examples of how the kingdom can become a scandal for us.

✤ *The treasure of eternal life is given without our seeking it.*

This parable is a counterpoint to the parable of the workmen in the vineyard. We saw there that the kingdom comes as sheer gift. We do not earn it, but receive it. This parable reminds us that once we have received the kingdom, we must assume the responsibility to share it with others. From this perspective, the parable is similar to the parable of the talents, in which one of those to whom the householder entrusted his

84

money hid it in the ground instead of taking the risk of putting it out at interest. He was condemned as a worthless servant.

Notice the subtlety of this teaching. This God of ours, like the father of the prodigal son, is always taking us back no matter what we do. God's largesse is boundless. But that very goodness involves a risk. The risk is that we treat the divine mercy as cheap grace, because we have done nothing to seek it or to earn it.

✤

In the mythologies of the various world cultures, the hero is always put to a test before he gets the treasure, the beautiful girl, the Holy Grail, or whatever the reward of the heavy trial. The hero has to slay the dragon to get into the cave or wherever the treasure is sequestered. All of those myths suggest that we do not access the greatest treasures of life without seeking for them ardently and passing through enormous tests. Having been through the appropriate test, we can then handle the treasure.

In Christianity the risk is that the treasure of eternal life is given without our seeking it. It is already there. The kingdom is among us and within us. It is a treasure that involves our participation in the divine life, to which no other conceivable good can compare.

❖Faith penetrates the psychological experience of prayer and the ups and downs of everyday life.

And for all practical purposes, most people are not interested. Thus if one receives it at the eleventh hour without having borne the heat of the day, the gift may not be adequately valued. Or if it is highly valued, we may make use of it in worldly ways for personal gain, whether for material profit, as in the case of the man in Thomas's Gospel, or simply by burying it so that no one else can get it.

Finding a treasure exempts us from everyday life. That is why this man experienced such joy, the joy of coming upon a great treasure without having to look for it and without having to work for it. Everyday life for most people requires earning a living. The treasure dispenses us from that. In the parables, the miracle is always muted and usually involves only moderate success after a string of failures. In the parable of the man who sower, as we saw, we hear about three dismal failures before the seed finally begins to take root and grow. But the final success of the seed consists in an ordinary harvest, not the superabundant and grandiose harvest that would go with the popular idea of the kingdom of God as triumphant.

The gospel reminds us that what takes us out of everyday life is hazardous. The grandiose appeals to our worldly programs for happiness. But the kingdom is not there. It is not in the lottery, even if we win. People love miracles and the extraordinary. The real response to this treasure is to discover the God of everyday, the God of the ordinary, the God who manifests the kingdom in the unclean and what may seem in our judgment to be scandalous.

When the spiritual journey becomes an inner treasure, we want to give more time to prayer, silence, and solitude. We do not want to be disturbed by the cares of the world. There is nothing wrong with this desire in due proportion, but to try to maintain our own peace of mind for selfish reasons, such as avoiding the problems of others, is to fail to understand the chief responsibility of the kingdom.

⁜

The parable of the hidden treasure reminds us of what can happen if we treat the free gift of the kingdom as something just for ourselves, or something that dispenses us from the duties of ordinary daily life and the labor of finding God's kingdom in it. In sharing the treasure of the kingdom, one increases one's grasp of it. The kingdom dissolves the monumental illusion that God is somehow absent from our lives or from our prayer. Faith penetrates the psychological experience of prayer and the ups and downs of everyday life, and keeps us directed toward God in the midst of all that happens. This is to respond to the treasure freely given. If we make some mistakes, we are not to let that bother us, not even if we make a fiasco of our whole life. God is not interested in vindicating rights, but in persuading us to be merciful to each other. The Father, whom Jesus reveals, loves us without any conditions and without ever getting tired of receiving us back when we fail.

GOD KNOWS
NO BOUNDARIES

Sixteen

THE GOOD SAMARITAN

"A MAN WAS GOING DOWN *from Jerusalem to Jericho, and fell into the hands of robbers, who stripped him, beat him, and went away, leaving him half dead. Now by chance a priest was going down that road; and when he saw him, he passed by on the other side. So likewise a Levite, when he came to the place and saw him, passed by on the other side. But a Samaritan while traveling came near him; and when he saw him, he was moved with pity. He went to him and bandaged his wounds, having poured oil and wine on them. Then he put him on his own animal, brought him to an inn, and took care of him. The next day he took out two denarii, gave them to the innkeeper, and said, 'Take care of him; and when I come back, I will repay you whatever more you spend.'" (Luke 10:30–35)*

To understand the full meaning of the parable of the good Samaritan, we need to be aware of the Jewish hierarchical society of the time. The priest, the Levite, and the ordinary Israelite or layperson were the familiar triad of that society. Sacred persons, places, and things were rigorously separated from the profane. Those who belonged to Israel—insiders—were sharply distinguished from those who were not—outsiders.

Samaritans were not only looked upon as outsiders, but as the mortal enemies of the nation of Israel and apostates from the Jewish religion. They derived from the northern tribes of Israel and had split off from the rest of the nation during King David's reign. A rabbinical text of the time states that "one who eats the food of Samaritans is eating the food of swine," thus equating Samaritans as apostates from Judaism. For this parable's original audience, a Samaritan was the epitome of ultimate corruption.

As the parable begins, we hear that a traveler from Jerusalem to Jericho, presumably an Israelite, has been beaten up by robbers and left half dead by the roadside. Along come the various representatives of the hierarchical structure of that society. A priest sees the man and passes by. A Levite, a step down on the hierarchical ladder, also passes by.

The reason why the first two pass by the victim is not addressed. The law commanded that priests and Levites were not to bury the dead apart from their next of kin. But in this case the man was "half dead," so they had no excuse to pass him by. The hearers would not be likely to identify with these two people and their merciless conduct. But neither would they be inclined to identify with the victim who was beaten up. The buildup of suspense focuses on who the next person coming down the road is going to be. Given the values of the Jewish society of the time, it has to be an Israelite layperson who will appear in the role of hero and bind up the wounds of the injured man. Then the hearers can all go home reinforced in their cultural mindsets.

The plot is designed to encourage the expectation of an Israelite savior. But who shows up coming down the road? A Samaritan, the mortal enemy of the Jewish nation and religion.

✠

To get an idea of how shocking this reversal of expectations would be for the original hearers, you may recall a movie entitled *Guess Who's Coming to Dinner?* In this film one of the principals is an editor of a liberal newspaper and a vigorous promoter of civil rights. His wife is in complete sympathy with his liberal views. They have a beautiful daughter upon whom they both dote and who dotes on them. One day the daughter announces that she has met a marvelous young man and that they have just become engaged. She expatiates loud and long on how much he is in full accord with all the social issues to which her father and mother are devoted. The parents are excited and say, "Well, bring him to dinner! We want to meet him!"

When the appointed day arrives and the engaged couple come to the door, the daughter rushes in first and embraces her beloved parents exclaiming, "I just can't wait till you meet him!" The audience has been built up to the same high pitch of expectancy to which the hearers of the parable were led before the appearance of the Samaritan. In this case, the parents are expecting a wonderful new addition to the family, one who will support their intense social concerns and projects. As the camera focuses on the entrance, in strides a tall, strapping, handsome black man, all smiles and ready to plunge into the arms of his prospective in-laws.

The camera then switches to the parents. We see the delighted expression on their faces fade with the suddenness of night descending in a deep canyon. The event has triggered something very unsettling for them. It is clear that on the conscious level they are very concerned about civil rights and social issues, but on the unconscious level their emotional values are being suddenly and severely confronted. This scene immediately raises the question, Just how open are they to equality with the black race? Clearly not to the point of welcoming a black man into the family. Their own identification and emotional investment in the values engendered in them by their cultural conditioning has been hidden from them until now. On the conscious level they are all for civil rights. On the unconscious level they are not prepared to accept the possibility of cross-cultural grandchildren. The moment of truth having arrived, they react with horror. From the perspective of their deepest emotional values, the young man represents monumental corruption. The unexpected often shows us what our secret values really are.

✤

To return to the parable of the good Samaritan, the hearers of Jesus' story are eagerly waiting to see who the next traveler is going to be on the road to Jericho. The clever design of the narrative has eased them into the expectation that it will be an Israelite layperson, on the lowest rung on the social ladder but still one of their own and hence acceptable. To their horror, the next traveler turns out to be a Samaritan! After the shock their first thought is, "He will surely finish off the poor guy!"

The Samaritan, however, starts ministering to the wounded man, pouring oil and wine into his wounds. He takes the injured man to an inn and pays for his stay. There the story ends, leaving the hearers without anybody in the story with whom to identify. They cannot identify with the priest, the Levite, or the victim, and it is inconceivable for most of them to identify with the Samaritan. That would be to accept the compassion and service of their mortal enemy. An impossible choice! For these hearers, the story must simply be untrue or makes no sense.

The message that is being communicated in this parable is that the kingdom of God knows no political or religious boundaries. The old maps of Israelite society are not relevant in this new kingdom. In the kingdom that Jesus is preaching, there are no rigid barriers between insiders and outsiders. More striking still, the temple in Jerusalem, center of the sacred in the popular mind, is no longer the sole criterion for holiness. In the person of the good Samaritan, the former universally accepted and unquestioned social and religious boundaries are swept away.

A favorite practice of the ancient Mediterranean cultures was to set up criteria for deciding who was in and who was out. In the kingdom revealed by Jesus, there is no way of deciding who is an insider and who is an outsider. This teaching must have sounded incredible for the people of that time who knew no other categories of judgment than the accepted social and religious distinctions. The great insight of early Christianity was that the kingdom of God is open to everyone. As Paul stated it, "There is no longer any distinction between Jew and Gentile, slave or free, male or female." The kingdom of God is open to everyone.

✤ *We are forced to acknowledge the goodness of those we detest or distrust.*

The movie described earlier is a modern parable dealing with basically the same issue. The implications of Jesus' teachings are especially apt in our time, because humanity is moving toward a global society with interaction among peoples in every conceivable way: economic, social, political, religious. The interiorization of Jesus' teaching about the unity of the human family as the most urgent expression of the will of God, must upstage every other value and consideration. Otherwise, violence, denial, and hypocrisy will abound.

The Samaritan in the parable was not rewarded. The kingdom of God is manifested in showing love whether or not it is accepted or its compassion appreciated. Divine love is its own reward. It is also irresistible. It keeps flowing until it finds someone who will receive it.

Would the first hearers of Jesus ever have understood the kingdom of God unless the one who came down the road was a Samaritan instead of the expected

Israelite? And will we ever overcome our various forms of denial unless we are confronted by opposition or tragedy? The kingdom of God may be most active in what is most unacceptable to us, such as the dark side of our personality and the humiliation of acknowledging our mixed motivation at work even in

✢ *The kingdom of God is open to everyone.*

our best intentions and in the service of others. Grace brings us to an ever-increasing awareness that under certain circumstances, we are capable of every evil. If the circumstances of our lives were challenged by starvation, serious illness, or a certain level of competition for money, prestige, position, love, or power, what would we actually do?

The Samaritan represents what we identify as monumental corruption. Our unquestioned values are profoundly undermined. We are forced to acknowledge the goodness of those we detest or distrust—perhaps even to accept compassionate service from them. The kingdom of God seeks to enter our lives just as they are. God wants us to show mercy, to take down doors, windows, and useless barriers of every kind. This is the message of the Samaritan, of the person or event that appears to us to be unmitigated evil—the master disguise in which God enters our lives in the fullest possible manner.

Jesus' parables leave the hearers with unresolved questions. The parable of the good Samaritan asks the question, "What is your idea of the kingdom of God?" Jesus' idea of the kingdom did not match the popular one of his time. In his view, the social map of first-century Palestinian culture is no longer a suitable vehicle for transmitting the kingdom of God.

Where does that leave the hearer? Perhaps with the question, "Do I want to live in this kingdom?"

To enter into the kingdom of God is to move beyond social expectations. Jesus identifies the action of the kingdom with the compassion of the Samaritan. The fact that the Samaritan is not converted suggests that the kingdom is not limited to religious attitudes or mindsets. Moreover, our supposed enemy may turn out to be our greatest benefactor.

According to this parable the kingdom of God has no fixed social, ethnic, racial, nationalistic, economic, or religious boundaries. There are no insiders or outsiders, no elite or nonelite. The abba whom Jesus reveals is the God of the human race as a family. Everyone must be concerned about everyone else. Unconditional love is the name of the game.

THE PRODIGAL SON 2

"THERE WAS A MAN WHO HAD TWO SONS. *The younger of them said to his father, 'Father give me the share of his property that will belong to me.' So he divided the property between them. A few days later the younger son gathered all he had and traveled to a distant country, and there he squandered his property in dissolute living. When he had spent everything, a severe famine took place throughout that country, and he began to be in need. So he went and hired himself out to one of the citizens of that country, who sent him to his fields to feed the pigs. He would gladly have filled himself with the pods that the pigs were eating; and no one gave him anything. But when he came to himself he said, 'How many of my father's hired hands have bread enough and to spare, but here I am dying of hunger! I will get up and go to my father, and I will say to him, "Father, I have sinned against heaven and before you; I am no longer worthy to be called your son, treat me like one of your* hired hands.'" So he set off and went to his father. But while he was still a far off, his father saw him and was filled with compassion; he ran and put his arms around him and kissed him. Then the son said to him, 'Father, I have sinned against heaven and before you; I no longer worthy to be called your son.' But the father said to his slaves, 'Quickly, bring out a robe—the best one—and put it on him; put a ring on his finger and sandals on his feet. And get the fatted calf and kill it, and let us eat and celebrate; for this son of mine was dead and is alive again; he was lost and is found.' And they began to celebrate.

"Now his elder son was in the field; and when he came and approached the house, he heard music and dancing. He called one of the slaves and asked what was going on. He replied, 'Your brother has come, and your father has killed the fatted calf because he has got him back safe and sound.' Then he became angry and refused to go in. His father came out and began to plead with him. But he answered his father, 'Listen! For all these years I have been working like a slave for you, and I have never disobeyed your command; yet you have never given me even a young goat so that I might celebrate with my friends. But when this son of yours came back, who has devoured your property with prostitutes, you killed the fatted calf for him!' Then the father said to him, 'Son, you are always with me, and all that is mine is yours. But we had to celebrate and rejoice, because this brother of yours was dead and has come to life; he was lost and has been found.'" (Luke 15:11–32)

This parable takes place in the context of a society where everyone was assigned a fixed place in the class structure. In that society a father was the representative of the law. The inheritance was of extreme importance and was governed by a legal code and maintained by strict rules. The father's role was to protect both the honor of the family and the inheritance. The inheritance could be divided prior to his death, but in this case it was the duty of the sons to set aside adequate funds to take care of him in his old age.

The story begins with the outrageous conduct of the younger son who demands his inheritance ahead of schedule and then, having received it, takes off for the good life. We hear about his progressive degradation. He finally winds up in disaster. A famine comes upon the country and he has nothing to eat. To avoid starving, he takes a job caring for pigs, an occupation that was considered apostasy from the Jewish religion. Eating pork was one of its religious taboos. In short, the prodigal hits bottom from every perspective.

The poverty of the prodigal is described in terms of a desperate lack of food. Nourishment belonged to the maternal function of this society, but there is no mother in the story. Maybe that was his problem. He is hungry and he recalls how well fed the servants were in his father's house. The thought comes, "I'll go back to my father's house. I won't ask to be his son. If only I can be one of the hired hands, I'll have something to eat."

He starts trudging back in his rags and smelling to high heaven of his charges in the pig sty. He has jeopardized the family's economic standing and put his father at risk by dissipating with foreigners that part of his inheritance that belonged by right to his father in his old age. Besides gross ingratitude, he has added the sin of injustice.

His father evidently has one eye on the road and is overwhelmed with boundless joy when he sees his ragamuffin son coming home. He dashes out and covers him with affectionate embraces and kisses. This free expression of love is totally out of character for a father in this patriarchal society. In the only other place in scripture where this term is used, Joseph "fell on his brothers' necks and kissed them affectionately" (Gen. 45:14–15).

Here, then, is a father who disregards his honor, the inheritance, and the patriarchal standards of the time, and acts like a mother. When the prodigal acknowledges his sin, the father does not even listen to his carefully prepared speech and the part about his becoming a hired hand. He immediately calls for the best robe, which is probably one of his own. He orders the servants to put sandals on his son's feet, a symbol of his full restoration to honor in the family. There is not the slightest questioning of his sincerity. Then the father calls for the fatted calf, and the music and dancing begin.

The elder son now appears. He has been faithfully serving his father on the land and working diligently for his share of the inheritance. The disappearance of the younger son has put his own share in jeopardy because now he is going to have to provide for his father's old age entirely out of his own resources. He has reason to be indignant at his younger brother and refers to him contemptuously as "that son of yours."

On the other hand, by refusing to go in to the party, the elder son sins against the fourth commandment, which requires him to honor his father. When his father graciously comes out to remonstrate with him, the elder son berates the old man for his goodness saying, "You have rewarded this son of yours who has not only wasted his share of the family fortune, but by living with prostitutes has risked the family blood line." Along with his offensive language, he dishonors both his father and his brother by refusing to take part in the celebration. Thus he has broken the legal code of the time just as much as the younger son, but in his own way.

✠

This parable is obviously intended to subvert one of the favorite themes in the Old Testament—namely, that of the chosen and the rejected. Because of the older son's misconduct toward the father, the hearers are expecting the story of Jacob and Esau to be repeated. Jacob, the younger son, was chosen by God while Esau, the elder son, to whom the inheritance legally belonged, was rejected. The expectation is that the elder son in this story is also going to be rejected, and the hearers, who would have identified by now with the younger son, can rejoice along with him in being God's specially chosen people.

The conduct of the father, however, effectively destroys the idea of Israel as the chosen people. Instead of rejecting the elder son for his disrespect, the father affirms, "You are always with me. Everything I have is yours." The elder son thus is assured of his share of the inheritance in spite of his misconduct. Just as the younger son is received back into the family in spite of dissipating his father's livelihood, so the elder son, who has just broken the fourth commandment by his insolent disrespect, is restored to favor. The father thus disregards the offenses of *both* sons. He puts completely aside his personal honor and the legal code. He shows himself equally disinterested in the immorality of his younger son and in the offensive self-righteousness that is the preoccupation of his elder son. Apparently the requirements of the Mosaic law are of no great importance to him. His conduct upstages both the misconduct of the younger son and the insistence on legal rights of the elder. The kingdom of God, it would seem from this parable, is

✢ *"You are always with me. Everything I have is yours."*

not primarily concerned with conventional morality or legalities. The father acts, according to the accepted standards of that society, as a bad father. However, as Scott puts it, he turns out to be a very good mother. Clearly this father unites in himself the qualities of both mother and father. The father in this parable represents the abba whom Jesus reveals as the God of infinite concern and love for all his children—that is, for the whole human family.

What emerges as the primary concern of the father in this parable? It is to unite his two sons: to bring them together in love. Both are guilty of serious failings and he wants to forgive them both. This father's chief concern is not justice but mercy. The father communicates unconditional love to his two sons so that they in turn may show mercy to each other. According to Jesus, his heavenly Father is not especially interested in legal codes and in conventional morality. He seeks the unity of the human family, the removal of divisions and barriers, and the triumph of compassion by manifesting the maternal values symbolized in that culture by nourishment and overflowing affection.

The parable must have left the Jewish audience with their mouths open in astonishment. What they thought was their major claim to God's protection and love, his free election of them as his chosen people, is profoundly undermined by this parable. The fact is that everyone is chosen. This includes both public sinners, who know that they have offended God, and the self-righteous who deny their complicity in sin. This father forgives both but commands them to live together in peace and common concern—the kind of concern that the Father has shown in sending his Son into the world as the sign of his forgiveness of everything and everyone.

LAZARUS AND
THE RICH MAN

"THERE WAS A RICH MAN *who was dressed in purple and fine linen and who feasted sumptuously every day. And at his gate lay a poor man named Lazarus, covered with sores, who longed to satisfy his hunger with what fell from the rich man's table; even the dogs would come and lick his sores. The poor man died and was carried away by the angels to be with Abraham. The rich man also died and was buried. In Hades, where he was being tormented, he looked up and saw Abraham far away with Lazarus by his side. He called out, 'Father Abraham, have mercy on me, and send Lazarus to dip the tip of his finger in water and cool my tongue; for I am in agony in these flames.' But Abraham said, 'Child, remember that during your lifetime you received your good things, and Lazarus in like manner evil things; but now he is comforted here, and you are in agony. Besides all this, between you and us a great chasm has been fixed, so that those who might want to pass from here to you cannot do so, and no one can cross from there to us.''' (Luke 16:19–26)*

In this parable, the sudden reversal of roles and expectations so characteristic of Jesus' teaching is once again manifested. Two extreme situations are juxtaposed. A rich man dressed in purple, symbol of the upper classes and power, feasted not just well, but sumptuously—and not just on feast days, but every day. At the gate to his estate lay Lazarus the beggar. In the popular mindset of the time beggars were considered responsible for their miserable plight. Poverty was looked upon as a punishment for sin and for that reason, the hearers would be thinking, "It's his own fault."

Lazarus dies and is carried by angels to Abraham's bosom, symbol of the fulfillment of all the promises made by God to Israel. The rich man also dies and is buried in Hades. In Jewish religious literature, prior to this time, there is no mention of a chasm between the just and the unjust that extends beyond the grave. This is a new note that the parable here introduces. Abraham responds to the rich man's plea by pointing out that he had enjoyed every good thing during his earthly life and now is in torment, while the poor man had experienced just the opposite.

The kingdom of God in Jesus' preaching presupposes solidarity with the community and its needs. In this light we begin to see what was wrong with this rich man's behavior. No particular misdeeds of his are listed. The parable indicates that it was not his wealth that was the cause of his undoing but his use of it. He failed to share with the community the abundance that God had given him. Such is the true purpose of the blessings of wealth. Thus this parable inveighs against the sin of indifference that fails to share one's abundance with those in need. It does so by juxtaposing the rich man's private enjoyment of his great abundance with the extreme want of the beggar for whom no practical concern was offered.

The sin of the rich man could not have been his wealth as such, since Abraham too was a rich man and found favor with God as the book of Genesis attests. The rich man's fate suggests that his sin was his failure to pass through the gate of his estate and to respond to the desperate need of the beggar. The parable attacks the complacency of our divisions between rich and poor, the socially acceptable and the socially outcast. The gate symbolizes the grace that enables us to love our neighbor—everyone—as ourselves. The rich man stayed in his enclosure. His failure to go through the gate and to enter into solidarity with the one in need was the particular cause of his undoing.

Gates can be barriers or passageways into solidarity with others. In whatever way the rich man obtained his goods, whether through junk bonds or other means of getting rich quick, he failed to pass through the gate of his private interests and concerns to identify with someone whose situation was desperate and whom he could easily have helped. In the next life things will be reversed. If the rich man had gone through the gate to reach out to the beggar and had not simply used it as a barrier to protect himself and his property, his fate would have been quite different. God does not set up barriers. We do. Our relationship to our local community and to the human family as a whole determines whether we are in the kingdom or out of it, both now and in the next life.

✥

To understand this teaching more clearly, let us look at a modern parable that seems to me to express in contemporary terms the main point of this parable. The classic movie, *Casablanca,* emphasizes what is meant by the word "solidarity" in this context. In the movie Rick, played by Humphrey Bogart, has a poignant romance with Ilsa, played by Ingrid Bergman, just before the German occupation of Paris in World War II. They agree to leave Paris on the last train. When she does not show up, his heart is broken. He has to leave to escape the Gestapo and winds up in Casablanca running a night club. Ilsa turns up one night at the night club with her husband who turns out to be the prime force in the underground of the French Resistance. Rick is completely undone by her reappearance in his life. After much misunderstanding she finally gets a chance to explain what happened.

✢ God does not set up barriers. We do.

When they had met in Paris, she had believed that her husband had been killed. When he turned up unexpectedly, on the very day she and Rick were to leave Paris, she had decided that her husband who was sick and in hiding needed her and that her first duty was to him. Hence her decision not to meet Rick at the train. But now she confesses, "I loved you then and I still love you!" And a little later, "I ran away from you once. I cannot do it again."

The hero of the French Resistance is being tracked down by the Gestapo. Rick has possession of two visas. Ilsa finds herself in a double bind: to stay with Rick or to escape with her husband. She tells Rick, "You must decide for both of us." As the plot unfolds, he makes the painful decision to put her and her husband on the plane while he stays behind.

In making this choice, Rick did precisely what the rich man in the parable failed to do. He passed through the gate of his own little world into solidarity with the whole human family. He put the desperate world situation of his time above his own happiness. He saw that the leader of the French Resistance, Ilsa's husband, was contributing to the undermining of Hitler's tyranny and that this heroic man needed the support of his wife in order to fulfill his role. He could have had Ilsa for himself, but he chose to let go of his private world with its alluring promise of personal happiness for the greater good of the whole human family. This is actually what God the Father has done according to the Christian faith, in sending his only begotten Son into the world to be crucified for our salvation. It is this insight into the heart of God and its manifestation in human affairs that makes this film so extraordinary.

Human love imitates divine love by joining the human family in its desperate needs.

✤

As we saw in the parable of the prodigal son, the father throws away his honor and personal interests in order to enter into solidarity with his disobedient sons. The kingdom of God is for everyone who understands that solidarity with the human family, made concrete in our local community, is the name of the game. Truly marvelous is the gate that enables us to enter into communion with one another. In that communion the kingdom of God achieves its highest activity. We are empowered to be and to act like God. On the other hand, if we use the gate to protect ourselves from those in need, the gate becomes a barrier that may continue into the next life.

Both parables speak of human love that imitates divine love by joining the human family in its desperate needs. If we are rich, our wealth is for the community, not for us. And if we love, our love must take into account an ever-increasing identification with everyone in the human family.

The nature of the kingdom of God is that it has to be shared. Hence in the Christian perspective, community is the supreme value. To relate to the whole human family as God's family is the basic thrust of the gospel. That is why the refusal to be reconciled is such a serious matter and why, when Peter asked, "How many times must I forgive?" Jesus replied with a symbolic number meaning "without end." That is the proper way to love our neighbor as ourselves.

To be in the kingdom is to participate in God's solidarity with the poor by sharing with them the good things that have been given to us. In the New Testament the great sin is to be deaf to the cry of the poor whether that cry springs from emotional, material, or spiritual need. Although we cannot help but partake in some degree in social injustice because we live in this world, we must constantly reach out in concrete and practical ways to those in need. Divine love is not a feeling, but a choice. It is to show mercy. The rich man, although he saw the beggar starving at his doorstep and could easily have reached out to him, just went on eating, drinking, and reading his *Wall Street Journal.*

Nineteen

THE GREAT DINNER

"SOMEONE GAVE A GREAT DINNER *and invited many. At the time for dinner he sent his slave to say to those who had been invited, 'Come, for everything is ready now.' But they all alike began to make excuses. The first said to him, 'I have bought a piece of land, and I must go out and see it; please accept my regrets.' Another said, 'I have bought five yoke of oxen, and I am going to try them out; please accept my regrets.' Another said, 'I have just been married and therefore I cannot come.' So the slave returned and reported this to his master. Then the owner of the house became angry and said to his slave, 'Go out at once into the streets and lanes of the town and bring in the poor, crippled, the blind, and the lame.' And the slave said, 'Sir, what you have ordered has been done, and there is still room.' Then the master said to the slave, 'Go out to the roads and lanes, and compel people to come in, so that my house may be filled.'" (Luke 14:16b–23)*

There are three accounts of this parable: one from Matthew, one from Luke, and one from the Gospel of Thomas. In Matthew's Gospel, the householder becomes a king. It is part of Matthew's allegory that those who do not come to this party will get the cold shoulder in the future. In Luke the householder takes revenge on those who insulted him by refusing his invitation. In all these versions, the great dinner is the symbol of the kingdom of God. Those who come to the meal receive salvation, and those who decline are rejected.

Why do all three traditional accounts make such a big deal about those who decline? For one thing, they all offer rather lengthy excuses, all of which are somewhat lame. In a village culture, one's honor was all-important and depended on one's acceptance by one's peers. Attendance at an important dinner party was one such symbol of acceptance. All those originally invited lived in houses and hence belonged to the upper classes. Since the first two invitations failed, the expectation of the hearers is that the third will be accepted. In the parable of the good Samaritan, the first two travelers pass by and the third turns out to be merciful. In the parable of the talents, the first two servants are well received and the third is rejected.

The fact that in this parable all three invitations are refused, emphasizes the total rejection of the householder and the utter shame that he suffers from his peers. The disgrace of the householder seems to have caused the three versions of the parable to lose something of their original force. The evangelists provide opportunities for the householder to regain his honor (if not to get his revenge) by rejecting the original invitees. The dinner, however, continues to represent the messianic banquet prophesied by Isaiah.

As the parable unfolds in Luke, when the householder is rejected by all his well-to-do peers in the village, he flies into a rage and orders his servants to go into the streets and bring in the lame, the blind, and the disabled. The invitation to the disabled suggests to the hearers of the time that the feast is a symbol of the messianic kingdom when all those who have been oppressed by diseases or by Israel's enemies will at last be raised up to an exalted stature and Israel's honor will be restored.

In the parable of the mustard seed, the hearers expected the seed to grow into a cedar of Lebanon (300 feet high) and instead it became a four-foot shrub. Here, instead of a glorious banquet, the house ends up full of undesirables and street people.

There is a progression: first come the disabled and the oppressed; afterward come the prostitutes, pickpockets, tax collectors, and all the disreputable riffraff of the town. These are the people who finally show up for the dinner.

✢

At this point the average hearer is quite uncomfortable. The prophetic text of Isaiah about the messianic banquet has been completely undermined. Let us recall the description of Isaiah:

> ON THIS MOUNTAIN THE LORD *of hosts will make for all peoples a feast of rich food, a feast of well-aged wines, of rich food filled with marrow, of well-aged wines strained clear. And he will destroy on this mountain the shroud that is cast over all peoples, the sheet that is spread over all nations; he will swallow up death forever. Then the Lord God will wipe away tears from all faces, and the disgrace of his people he will take away from all the earth, for the Lord has spoken. It will be said on that day, Lo, this is our God; we have waited for him, that he might save us. This is the Lord for whom we have waited; let us be glad and rejoice in his salvation.* (Is. 25:6–9)

The feast and the celebration of the meal in this text of Isaiah clearly symbolizes a mighty victory over the Lord's enemies. He will vanquish the ruthless nations and the oppressed people of God will be restored to honor by their all-powerful God. Such is the principal theme of the passage; the problem is that it does not happen in the parable.

❖

In the local villages of the time there was no chance for upward mobility. It was a closed society. Having been rejected by his peers, the householder has to choose between canceling the dinner or inviting others that he would never have thought of asking. In the messianic banquet foreseen by Isaiah, God raises the oppressed people to God's own status and destroys all their enemies. In Jesus' parable, the householder does not raise up the oppressed but joins them in their various forms of human misery. Instead of a vindictive triumph over Israel's enemies, the bottom line is that the kingdom of God as Jesus proclaims it is being celebrated with the destitute and with sinners.

In other words, the kingdom is to be found not in a dinner for the rich and famous, but in table fellowship with the poor, with people of no account, and with those who hang out on street corners. These are the people who in fact finally take part in the dinner. In this remarkable parable Jesus opens a window on the nature of his Father. The celebration of the salvation of God, symbolized by the dinner, is not taking place with the big shots, the well-to-do, and the successful—they declined—but is taking

✤ *God comes to those who consent to come to God with their lives just as they are.* place with the poor, the weak, the ignorant, the oppressed, and those afflicted with physical, emotional, and spiritual pain. That is, in soup kitchens, bread lines, ghettos, and in places where nobody wants to go.

The expectation of the hearers is completely subverted. Just as in the parable of the mustard seed, there is no cedar of Lebanon, so here there is no great dinner. It is our desperate need that attracts divine mercy, not our virtues or anything else.

✤

Can we accept a God who becomes so vulnerable as to join the human condition exactly where it is, or more precisely, exactly where we are—in the midst of our impure motivation and behavior? God comes to those who consent to come to God with their lives just as they are. The life and death of Jesus is the actual working out of what it means for God to become a human being.

THE NEW WINE

THEN THE DISCIPLES OF JOHN *came to him, saying, "Why do we and the Pharisees fast often but your disciples do not fast?" Jesus said to them, "The wedding guests cannot mourn as long as the bridegroom is with them, can they? The days will come when the bridegroom is taken away from them, and then they will fast. No one sews a piece of unshrunk cloth on an old cloak, for the patch pulls away from the cloak, and a worse tear is made. Neither is new wine put into old wineskins; otherwise, the skins burst, and the wine is spilled, and the skins are destroyed; but new wine is put into fresh wineskins, and so both are preserved." (Matthew 9:14–17)*

John the Baptist made quite a stir in Israel and attracted many disciples. Jesus was baptized by him and drew his first disciples from among John's followers. John was austere. He wore a loincloth and ate only locusts and wild honey. He practiced much fasting and expected the same of his disciples.

When there are two spiritual teachers or religious communities in the same neighborhood, the loyalties of one group may conflict with the loyalties of the other. There may be some mutual denigrating and backbiting. Comparisons may be made between *our* observance and their observance, *our* spiritual teacher and their spiritual teacher, *our* tradition and their tradition.

In this incident, John's disciples were sniping at the disciples of Jesus. They said, "How is it that the Pharisees and we fast and you folks do not?"—implying that Jesus' disciples were not measuring up to the high standards of John's. "Who are you" is the implication of the question, "compared with us?" An austere observance draws public attention, admiration, and acclaim.

✢ *The exuberance of the Spirit cannot be contained in the old structures.*

Jesus graciously adjusts himself to these human foibles. He responds with a question of his own, "How can the wedding guests go mourning while the bridegroom is with them?" By this question he implies that John's disciples are not seeing the whole picture. They are looking for holiness, but in the wrong place.

He adds, "When the bridegroom is taken away, then the wedding guests will fast."

He appeals to the fact that his presence among his disciples is a celebration and that it is not appropriate to mourn while attending a wedding. At the very least, they will not be welcome guests. A celebration requires the capacity to receive as well as to give. When God graciously comes into our lives for a few minutes, it is not the time to practice our customary austerities. It is like having a surprise visit from a dear relative who comes to share affection and love, and who finds us too busy with various chores to say anything but, "Come back some other time."

Jesus continues, "Nobody sews a piece of unshrunken cloth on an old cloak. That will only make the rip bigger." And he adds, "People do not pour new wine into old wineskins." An old wineskin dries out, shrivels, and cracks. If we put new wine into it, the chemicals that are still being processed in the new wine will burst the old skin. The old skin does not have the flexibility to expand with the effervescence.

New wine is a marvelous image of the Holy Spirit. As we move to the intuitive level of consciousness through contemplative prayer, the energy of the Spirit cannot be contained in the old structures. They are not flexible enough. They may have to be left aside or adapted. The new wine as a symbol of the Spirit has a tendency to stir people up; for that reason, the fathers of the church called it "sober intoxication." Although its exuberance is subdued, it breaks out of categories and cannot be contained in neat boxes.

Jesus points out to John's disciples that they have a good practice but are too attached to fasting as a structure. The wine of the Spirit that Jesus brings will not fit into their narrow ideas. They must expand their views. Otherwise, the new wine of the gospel will give them trouble. It will burst the narrow confines of their mindsets, and both what they have and what they are trying to receive will be lost.

Jesus suggests a solution: "Put the new wine into new wineskins." The new wine of the Gospel is manifested by the fruits of the Spirit, which, according to Gal. 5:22–24, are nine aspects of the mind of Christ. If the new wine is to be preserved, new structures have to be found that are more appropriate than the old ones. If we lean too heavily on the old structures, the new wine of the Spirit will be lost. This happened in the late Middle Ages and especially in the post-Reformation Catholic Church when the emphasis moved from cultivating the fruits of the Spirit to conformity to doctrinal formulas and external observances. That is why we found ourselves at the time of Vatican II in a spiritual desert. The old wine had run out. Renewal in the Spirit, the new wine, is our recovery of the contemplative tradition of Christianity. But this movement of the Spirit has to be put into new structures; the old ones are likely to burst.

Is it possible to renovate old wineskins? With a lot of greasing they may regain some flexibility, but not as much as new ones. The process may also take a long time.

❖

What will happen with the renewal of contemplative life among lay folks? We will see new forms of contemplative lifestyles that better serve the new wine with its tendency to expand, to excite, and to go to one's head, so to speak. The new wine is the contemplative dimension of the gospel. Its basic act is consent to the presence and action of the Spirit within us. This consent is directed not to our intentionality but to God's intentionality. The Spirit who loves us first is pouring the wine, not we. It is a mistake to think that we have to win God's attention or impress God with our virtues. That is not the new wine. That is an attitude that belongs to the old wine where our virtues are viewed as the necessary means of winning God's favor.

If we consent to God's intentionality, God works in us through the fruits of the Spirit: boundless compassion, joy, peace, and the others enumerated by Paul. No structure can contain such wine. Paul adds, "Those who are moved by the Spirit have no Law." They are beyond any law because they fulfill the purpose of all laws, which is the continuous flow of divine love and compassion. Thus they fulfill every just law spontaneously.

THE COMING OF THE KINGDOM

In the parable of the great dinner, the original people invited did not take their invitation seriously. A
similar problem is treated in the parable of the hidden
treasure. If we get something for nothing, we tend
not to value it too highly. This is the risk that God
has taken in inviting us to share the divine life.

In the parable of the great dinner, a symbol of the
kingdom of God, we would expect that the householder would get huffy and say, "Since my friends
and peers won't come, to heck with the banquet!"
He does in fact get very annoyed at the original invitees who did not value his invitation. But rather than
cancel the affair, he tells his servants to go out and
bring in the lame, the halt, and the blind. Even then
the banquet hall is not filled. As a final effort, he sends
his servants out to beat the bushes, so to speak, and
bring in anyone they can find, the street people and

public sinners. These are the people who actually take part in the banquet. The householder shares the meal with them. Evidently God does not stand on honor but prefers to identify with us and enter into our ordinary lives and deaths, including the scandalous elements in our lives that the leaven in the parable of the leaven symbolizes.

In this way God reveals solidarity with us in the ordinary affairs of daily life, as well as in times and places of monumental corruption whether this be physical disaster, mental illness, or moral degradation. Jesus exemplified the latter by eating and drinking with sinners, which was in his time the sign of belonging to the group with whom one shared table fellowship. The more desperate the need, the more the infinite mercy of God responds by living it with us if we consent.

Christian transmission, then, is not a revelation leading to high states of enlightenment but a participation in the mind of Christ. In this transmission the community—family, local, national, global, the entire universe—is all-important. God is interested in the salvation of every human being and wants us, above every other consideration, to get along together in peace and harmony. If we can believe the teaching implied in Jesus' parables, morality is rooted in this primary concern, and in laws and rules only insofar as they lead to and support the disposition of unconditional love. This understanding is exemplified in the parable of the prodigal son in which both sons treated their father abominably. He forgave them both without putting either of them to any test of repentance. The transmission of divine life is designed to empower us to think, act, and feel as God does, or at least as God would think, act, and feel if God were a human being. As things are, we have to do that for God.

ADDITIONAL COPYRIGHT
INFORMATION

Fr. Thomas Keating, O.C.S.O.
(1923-2018)

Fr. Thomas Keating was a Trappist monk and one of the most vocal and inspiring leaders of modern Christian contemplation. He helped develop new contemplative practices now widely used around the world, and a psychology of the spiritual journey. As founder of Contemplative Outreach, Fr. Thomas gathered people of all walks of life for the practice of centering prayer and the advancement of contemplative lifestyles. Fr. Thomas served as abbot of his monastic community, founded the Snowmass Interreligious Conference, and served as president of the Temple of Understanding and of the Monastic Interreligious Dialogue. Author of numerous books, Fr. Thomas traveled the world to give workshops, teach and meditate with others.

About the Publisher

The Crossroad Publishing Company publishes Crossroad and Herder & Herder books. We offer a 200-year global family tradition of books on spiritual living and religious thought. We promote reading as a time-tested discipline for focus and understanding. We help authors shape, clarify, write, and effectively promote their ideas. We select, edit, and distribute books. With our expertise and passion, we provide wholesome spiritual nourishment for heart, mind, and soul through the written word.